First Encyclopedia of Seas & Oceans

Ben Denne

Designed by Nelupa Hussain
and Helen Wood

Illustrated by David Hancock

Consultants: Dr. Margaret Rostron, Dr. John Rostron,
John Davidson and H.M. Hignett

SCHOLASTIC INC.
New York Toronto London Auckland
Sydney Mexico City New Delhi Hong Kong

Usborne Quicklinks

The Usborne Quicklinks Website is packed with links to the best websites on the internet. For links and downloadable pictures for this book, go to:

www.usborne-quicklinks.com
and enter the keywords **"first seas"**

You'll find links to websites where you can:

- Take a journey to the bottom of the ocean
- Watch videos of sea creatures in their habitats
- Search for sunken treasure
- Test your knowledge with undersea quizzes

Downloadable pictures
You can download lots of the pictures in this book and use them in your projects. All the pictures marked with a ★ are available to download at the Usborne Quicklinks Website.

Internet safety guidelines
When using the internet please follow the internet safety guidelines displayed on the Usborne Quicklinks Website.

Contents

Seas and oceans

More than two-thirds of the Earth is covered with salty water. This makes the planet look blue from space.

The water is divided into five large areas called oceans. In some places these are divided into smaller areas called seas.

Watery world

It is like a different world under the oceans. There are deep valleys, huge mountains, forests of seaweed and many amazing sea animals.

Internet links

For links to websites with games and activities about the ocean, go to **www.usborne-quicklinks.com** and type in the keywords "first seas".

Coast

Oil platform

Divers only go down to about 150m (500ft). The deepest parts of the oceans may be more than 80 times deeper than this.

Most oceans have a shallow area near the coast.

Oil gets trapped between layers of rock under the sea.

People drill holes into the seabed to get the oil out. See page 51 to find out more.

At the bottom of the sea is the seabed.

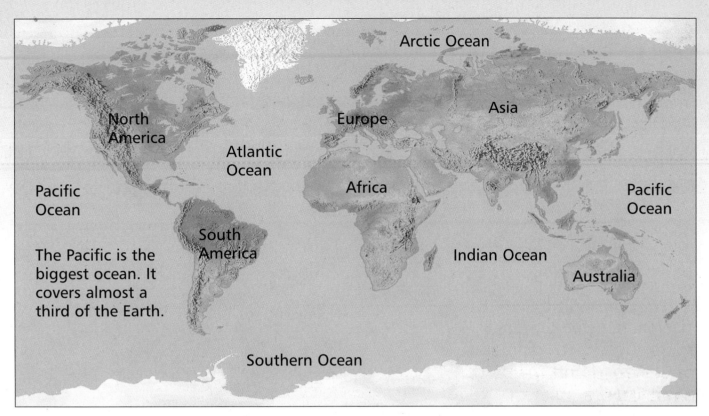

Arctic Ocean

Asia

Europe

North America

Atlantic Ocean

Africa

Pacific Ocean

Pacific Ocean

The Pacific is the biggest ocean. It covers almost a third of the Earth.

South America

Indian Ocean

Australia

Southern Ocean

This map shows the five different oceans. Remember that the world is round, so the two parts of the Pacific Ocean join up.

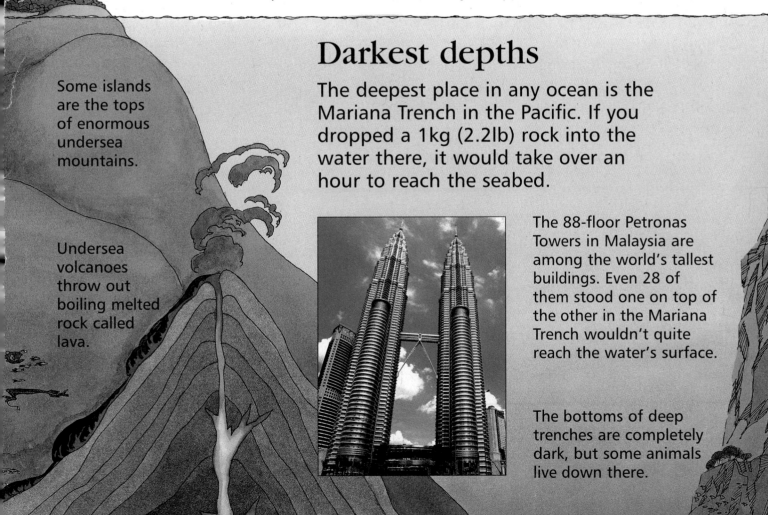

Darkest depths

Some islands are the tops of enormous undersea mountains.

The deepest place in any ocean is the Mariana Trench in the Pacific. If you dropped a 1kg (2.2lb) rock into the water there, it would take over an hour to reach the seabed.

Undersea volcanoes throw out boiling melted rock called lava.

The 88-floor Petronas Towers in Malaysia are among the world's tallest buildings. Even 28 of them stood one on top of the other in the Mariana Trench wouldn't quite reach the water's surface.

The bottoms of deep trenches are completely dark, but some animals live down there.

5

Underwater life

The oceans are full of living things. Some sea creatures are gentle and friendly, but others are fierce hunters.

Internet links

For links to websites where you can find out all about life underwater, go to **www.usborne-quicklinks.com** and type in the keywords "first seas".

Most types of shark are deadly hunters. They have sharp teeth for eating other animals.

Dolphins are one of the most intelligent and playful kinds of sea animal.

Coral reefs are beautiful underwater structures. They are home to many different sea animals.

Sea slugs collect other animals' poison and use it themselves against their enemies.

What are fish?

Fish are a group of animals that live in water. There are thousands of different kinds. They come in different shapes and sizes, but they all have gills and fins. Gills allow them to breathe under water, and fins help them to move around.

Caudal fin

Most fish have flat tails, which they move from side to side to swim. Their strong tail muscles make swimming easy.

Fish use these top fins, called dorsal fins, to help keep their balance.

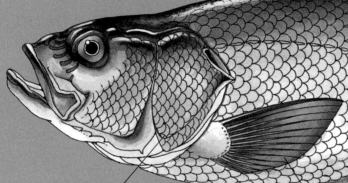

This flap, called the operculum, covers the fish's gills.

Slimy skin helps fish to move easily through water.

Fish use these fins, called pectoral fins, for turning.

This line, called the lateral line, helps fish to sense movement in the water.

Pelvic fins help fish to change direction quickly.

Breathing

Fish breathe by taking oxygen out of the water. Here's how they do it.

Gills under here

As a fish moves forward, it takes in water through its mouth. The water passes over its gills.

The fish's gills take oxygen from the water. The water then passes out under the fish's operculum.

Fish scales

Most fish are protected by a covering of tiny plates, called scales. These scales are waterproof, and help to protect the fish from pests and hunters.

Fish scales overlap each other, to make a protective cover.

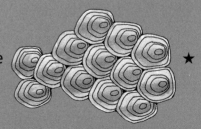

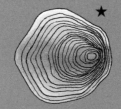

The rings on a fish's scales show how old the fish is. Some fish can live for up to 80 years.

Who eats who?

The animals in the oceans depend on each other to survive. Some animals eat plants, but some hunt and eat other animals.

Hunters and hunted

Animals which hunt and eat other animals are known as predators. The animals that they eat are called prey.

This killer whale is a predator. It is hunting mackerel. The mackerel are its prey.

Drifting plankton

Plankton are animals and plants which provide food for lots of other animals. There are billions of them in the oceans. They cannot swim, so they drift through the water. Most kinds of plankton are tiny.

Tiny plants in the water, such as these diatoms, are called phytoplankton.

One glass of sea water can contain as many as 50,000 phytoplankton.

These zooplankton animals are shown larger than they really are. In real life, most of them are actually smaller than one of the letters in these words.

Web of life

Food webs, like this one, show who eats who. The arrows point from the prey to the predators. Most predators are also prey for other, bigger animals. Predators which aren't eaten by other animals are called top predators.

Which are the top predators in this web?

Killer whale

Humpback whale

Tuna ★

★ Herring

Mackerel

★ Zooplankton

Phytoplankton ★

New from old

When animals are eaten by other animals, they pass on energy. Even if they die of old age, the energy is still passed on through the food web. When they die, animals help create new life. Follow the numbers to see how this happens.

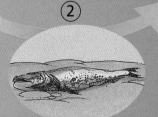

4. Plankton use the nutrients to build their bodies, which sea animals eat before they die.

④

①

②

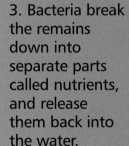
③

1. When a sea animal dies, it sinks to the seabed and gets covered in mud.

2. In the mud are tiny living things called bacteria. They feed on the remains of the dead animal.

3. Bacteria break the remains down into separate parts called nutrients, and release them back into the water.

Internet links

For links to websites where you can find out more about food webs, go to **www.usborne-quicklinks.com**.

Hiding

Many sea animals are difficult to spot because the patterns on their bodies look like their surroundings. This is called camouflage. Camouflage helps animals to hide when they are in danger. It can also help predators sneak up on prey.

Sea dragons have lots of leafy parts on their bodies, to make them look like seaweed.

Wobbegong sharks have flat bodies. They lie on the seabed, and snap up fish that swim past.

Flatfish disguise

Some flatfish use the seabed for camouflage. They cover themselves in sand and lie very still so they won't be seen.

Can you see the fish in this picture?

Safe spines

Shrimpfish hide by hanging head-down among the spines of sea urchins. The stripes along the sides of their bodies make them look like one of the sea urchin's spines. This protects them from predators.

Can you see the shrimpfish hiding on this sea urchin?

Changing patterns

Cuttlefish hunt on the seabed, eating fish and crabs. They have long tentacles which dart out to catch their prey. As they pass over different areas, their body pattern changes completely, to match their surroundings.

This cuttlefish is camouflaged against the sand.

As it moves over some rocks, its pattern changes.

Fierce frogfish

Sargassum frogfish live in areas of floating sargassum seaweed. Their bodies are perfectly camouflaged to look like the seaweed. They stay very still, and wait for their prey to swim close to them.

A sargassum frogfish can use its front fins like hands to cling to the seaweed.

Drilling for oil

Internet links

To find out more about using the oceans, go to **www.usborne-quicklinks.com** and type in the keywords "first seas".

In some of the rocks under the seabed, there is lots of oil. Big companies use oil platforms to drill holes into the seabed and get it out. It is used as fuel for things such as cars, factories and power stations.

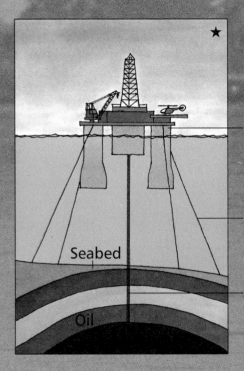

★ Floating oil platform

These floats stop the platform from sinking.

Cables with anchors on them stop the platform from moving.

Seabed

This pipe goes into the seabed as far as the oil. The oil is then pumped up.

Oil

Food, jewels and medicines

We get a lot more than just food and energy from the oceans. Here are some of the other things that come from the sea.

Mother-of-pearl covers the inside of abalone shells. It is used to decorate things.

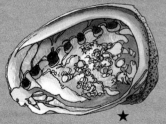 ★

Pearls are found inside animals called oysters. They are used to make necklaces and earrings.

 ★

Some kinds of seaweed are good to eat. Seaweed is also used to make shampoo and ice cream. ★

Some medicines come from the sea. Horseshoe crabs' blood is used to test for diseases. ★

Dirty oceans

The oceans are getting dirtier and dirtier because of things people dump in them. Our waste kills sea plants and animals. Here are some of the different ways people harm the oceans.

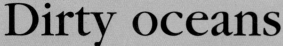

In some places, sewage pipes take waste from bathrooms and toilets and dump it into the sea.

Many farmers use chemicals to help their crops grow. When it rains, some of the chemicals are washed into rivers, and then into the sea.

Plastic dumped in the sea can take longer than 80 years to rot away.

Some ships dump their litter into the sea.

Some people leave litter behind on beaches. When the tide comes in, it is washed out to sea.

Oil spills

Huge oil tankers sometimes hit rocks or crash into other ships and oil leaks out into the sea. This can harm the sea and the animals that live in it.

Internet links

For links to websites where you can learn more about threats to the oceans, go to **www.usborne-quicklinks.com** and type in the keywords "first seas".

Seabirds get oil stuck in their feathers. When they try to clean it off with their beaks, it poisons them.

Some spilled oil floats on top of the water.

Oil tankers carry enormous amounts of oil. A big oil spill can cover a huge area.

When oil washes up on beaches, it sticks to the sand and pebbles and kills the plants and animals along the seashore.

Cleaning up

Cleaning up after an oil spill is a difficult job. People have to catch and clean the oily animals. Then they release them away from the oil.

This oil-covered seal is being cleaned with dishwashing liquid.

Emptying the oceans

As well as making the oceans dirty, we damage them in other ways. When we take too much from the oceans, it puts the animals and plants that live in them in danger.

Overfishing

When fishermen catch too many of the same kind of fish, the number in the sea starts to go down. This is called overfishing.

Modern fishing boats make catching fish much easier than it used to be.

Fishermen use helicopters to look for schools of fish.

Fishing controls

Some countries try to control the problem of overfishing. They make fishermen use special nets which only catch the larger fish.

The big holes in this fishing net allow small fish to escape.

Fish in danger

These fish are all in danger from overfishing. If fishermen don't stop catching them soon, they will die out completely.

Up to 70 million sharks are caught each year. Their fins are used to make soup. The rest is thrown away.

Small fish, such as haddock, are overfished.

Cod can grow up to 1.5m (5ft) long, but there are almost no big cod left, because of overfishing.

Pacific salmon have been overfished.

Millions of bigeye tuna are caught each year to make a Japanese food called sushi.

Coral in danger

Coral reefs are being damaged all over the world. Reefs grow slowly. Every reef that people damage will take hundreds of years to grow again.

★ Fishermen use poison to catch tropical fish from reefs. They sell them to pet shops.

People take coral to make things such as necklaces.

Coral is often damaged by careless divers.

55

Getting warmer

Many scientists think the Earth's temperature is slowly rising. As it gets warmer, the sea level will rise. The ocean currents and weather patterns may also change.

Trapped heat

The Earth is surrounded by a blanket of gases called the atmosphere. Some of these, called greenhouse gases, trap heat around the Earth, making it warm enough for life to exist. But people do some things that make extra gases. These trap more heat, so the Earth and its oceans get warmer.

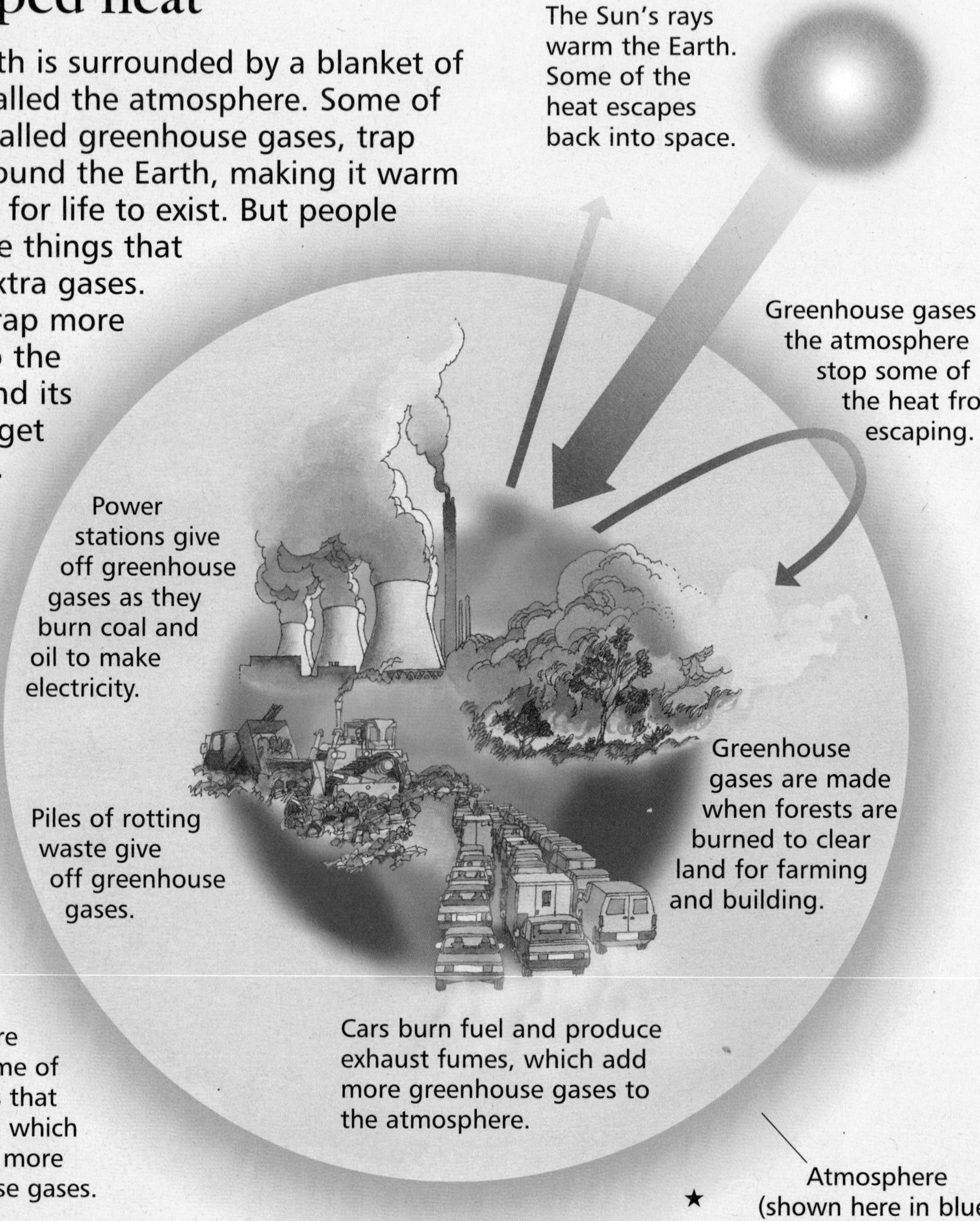

The Sun's rays warm the Earth. Some of the heat escapes back into space.

Greenhouse gases in the atmosphere stop some of the heat from escaping.

Power stations give off greenhouse gases as they burn coal and oil to make electricity.

Greenhouse gases are made when forests are burned to clear land for farming and building.

Piles of rotting waste give off greenhouse gases.

This picture shows some of the things that people do which can make more greenhouse gases.

Cars burn fuel and produce exhaust fumes, which add more greenhouse gases to the atmosphere.

Atmosphere (shown here in blue)

Melting ice

As the atmosphere warms up, the ice in the Arctic and the Antarctic starts to melt. When free-floating sea ice melts, it only makes a slight difference to the sea level. This is because it is made of fresh water, which is less dense than salty sea water.

The air gets warmer.

Ice melts into the sea.

Rising seas

If the world's land ice melted, it would cause a worldwide disaster. The sea level everywhere would rise by more than 60m (200ft). To stop this from happening, we need to find ways of making energy without burning fuels such as oil and coal. Find out more on the next page.

This picture shows what would happen to a town by the sea if the sea level rose by 60m (200ft).

Many islands in the sea would be flooded if all the ice melted.

Internet links

For links to websites where you can play games and learn about global warming, go to **www.usborne-quicklinks.com** and enter the keywords "first seas".

As ice melts at the poles, huge chunks of it fall into the sea.

The future of the oceans

Fuels, such as oil, may one day run out, and anyway, using them harms the Earth. But there are ways of getting energy from the sea itself. In the future, we could get most of our energy from the sea, and even live in it.

Wind power

The surface of the sea is often windy. Big windmills, called wind turbines, could be attached to the seabed and used to make electricity from the wind.

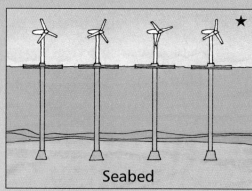

Seabed

Wind blowing across the sea turns the windmill blades.

The spinning blades power a machine called a turbine inside the windmill, which makes electricity.

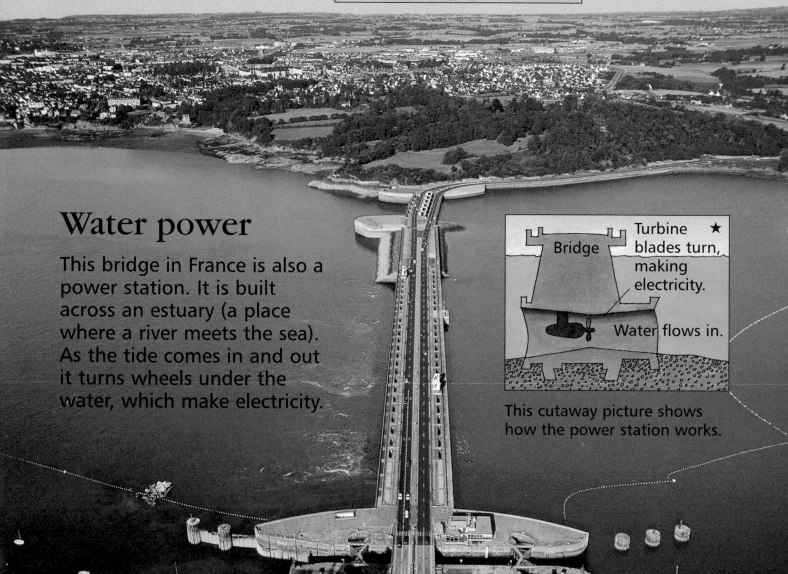

Water power

This bridge in France is also a power station. It is built across an estuary (a place where a river meets the sea). As the tide comes in and out it turns wheels under the water, which make electricity.

Bridge

Turbine ★ blades turn, making electricity.

Water flows in.

This cutaway picture shows how the power station works.

Living undersea

In the future, people could live in the oceans. A diver named Jacques Cousteau did some experiments in the 1960s, which showed that living under the sea was possible.

Kelp grows very quickly. People living undersea could farm it for food.

This is a picture of what an undersea village might look like.

People could enter their houses from the bottom.

Bars outside the entrances to undersea houses could keep out dangerous animals.

Internet links

For links to websites where you can find out more about the future of the oceans, go to **www.usborne-quicklinks.com**.

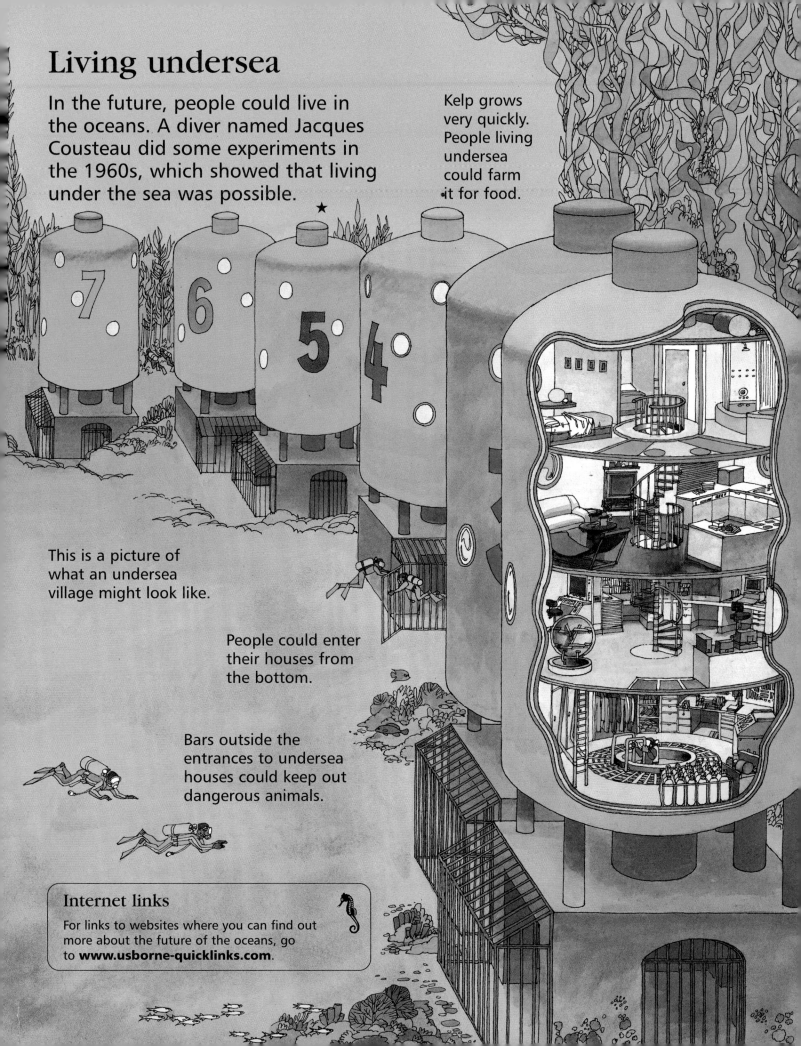

The glimmering, emerald-green net stretched out. Sunlight shining through the ice made it look like lace. Seeing the net dancing nearby, trout, whitefish, even pike, swam over to take a look.

Kwayus mithoonagasoo ana athapi meegwaach eepak'stawee-oot. Peesim eechaachaagoosit ita kaapaapooskoos'sit ana athapi, mitooni eewaawaasteepathik igoota oochi. Eewaap'-maachik athapeeya eenaaneemee-itoothit ataampeek igoota, nameegoosuk igwa ateega-meeg'wuk, apoochiga it'niginooseewuk, peetaatagaawuk, taaskooch eewaap'maachik.

When all the net had entered the lake, Papa and Cody set off for the second hole to catch the jigger when it arrived there. Ootsie leaped and barked beside them.

Ispeek kaagithow ana athapi eegeepak'stawee-oot, paapaa igwa Cody sipweepaataawuk igwa iteegee keetawm kaageepooskwa-oot maskwami, igoota tagaskeetaachik tagaachit'naachik anee-i chikara ispeek tagoopath'thichi. Kaagwaagwaaskootit igwa kaamaamiksimoot Ootsie ootaanaak paapaawa igwa Codeewa.

Suddenly, the sled dogs woke up. They had smelled a stranger.
On the other side of the lake sat a fox, her fur as bright as flames.
She sat perfectly still, sniffing the delicious lunch smells that
lingered in the air.

Kitaatawee kaawanskaapathichik atim'wuk. Eegeepasoochik
isa awithoowa. Agaameek neetee waathow kamateecheepatapit
peeyuk maageesees, oopeewaya eemeegwathigwow taaskooch
iskootao. Mawch waskawao. Igoota poogoo apoo eemaamithaatak
animeethoo meechoowin m'wees'chi igoospeek kaageemeechi-
naaniwuk neetee waathow wasagaam minstigook.

OR

A combination of full seasons and hours in either of the following ways:

     1 FULL SEASON Plus 330 hours.

     2 FULL SEASONS Plus 165 hours.

The restrictions regarding consecutive time and hours per week also apply.

OBJECTIVES OF THE CANADIAN AMATEUR SWIMMING ASSOCIATION'S LEVEL TWO TECHNICAL COURSE

"SWIMMING COACHING AT THE CLUB LEVEL" is the reference manual for the level II course of the Canadian Amateur Swimming Association's National Coaching Certification Program.

The purpose of the level II course is to develop the necessary ability and knowledge for a coach to be able to conduct a club program for swimmers with a range of proficiency from novice level up to — but not including — national championship qualifiers.

To achieve this **purpose**, the following **objectives** have been set for the level II program:—

A. The coach is able to provide a training program which:

   (1) EFFECTIVELY TRAINS THE APPROPRIATE ENERGY SYSTEMS used by swimmers in specific competitive events.

   (2) DEVELOPS STRENGTH, POWER, ENDURANCE AND FLEXIBILITY by means of safe, progressive supplementary land exercises.

   (3) DEVELOPS STROKE TECHNIQUE by using good communication and knowledge of hydrodynamics and skill-development methods.

   (4) MOTIVATES individual swimmers and the team by setting goals based on swimmers' motivations and abilities; using principles of effective communication; directing behavior by using appropriate reinforcement techniques.

   (5) ENSURES GOOD NUTRITION during training and competition by advising swimmers of good eating habits.

B. The Coach will understand the basic organization and administration required in a Canadian Swimming Club Program.

CONTENTS

the competitive event; setting schedules for various levels of ability; an outline of an early-season training program; an outline of a mid-season training program; sample of an eleven workout week for mid-season; comments on the eleven session week; swim all styles; use "descending series"; establish a balance between distance and sprint training; comments on distance training and sprint training; train the lactic acid system; learn to swim fast in morning workouts; combine short- and long-course workouts; other schedules for club workouts; late-season training; tapering; when to taper, tapering all aspects of the program. how to taper; a model for the tapering procedure (major meet); comments on the tapering plan; psychological preparation and tapering for major meets; schematic diagram on tapering all aspects of the training program.

split" swimming; stroke mechanics and swimming energy.

local meet; age-group meet; regional championships; provincial championships; trips at home and away; purpose of such trips.

Part Four — Motivation

PART ONE

TECHNIQUES

1 PRINCIPLES OF COMMUNICATION

Dr. Murray Smith,
Professor of Physical Education,
University of Alberta, Edmonton

PRINCIPLES OF COMMUNICATION

Coaching is communication. Much will be said about effective ways to communicate in the text on teaching strokes and skills, demonstrations, and questioning ("Teaching — Coaching Techniques"). The topic also is impossible to separate from any discussion of motivation, goal-setting, and reinforcement as discussed later. Careful attention to what is contained in those sections will assist better communication.

This section outlines other important aspects and re-emphasizes and extends a few of the ideas discussed earlier.

Plain language

While it is obvious that good verbal communication depends on using plain, understandable language, this simple rule is often overlooked. With younger children language is most important to reinforce and hold their attention and to focus it on whatever we want to teach them.

They need to **see what we are talking about** and **to do it**. As they **watch** and **do** they should be given the new words that apply to what they do. A common mistake is to use jargon terms that are like a foreign language to the newcomers. Instruction should depend **first** on what can be seen, demonstrated, tried out, and **described as** it is being done and **after** it is done.

Long descriptions of things before they are seen or done mean little to us regardless of our age. The rule should be **show or do and tell, not** tell and show.

It is helpful to observe children carefully, to sit and listen and watch them as they talk and play together. The coach can learn many useful things this way. Among them are how the kids think, what is important to them, who is important to them, and how they talk to each other; what language **they** use.

When instructing children or adults, the coach should be alert for puzzled looks, gestures, or reactions, such as glances between people that indicate confusion or disagreement, and be prepared to stop and try to find out the cause. Questions like, "Do you understand that? If not, let's talk about that a bit," or "Does that make sense?" will help.

Above all, the coach should be patient and decent in trying to help people understand. If the coach shows impatience, or in any way ridicules those who do not understand or who ask questions or show bewilderment, honest questions will be stifled. The pupils will either try to hide their ignorance or become very annoyed or resentful because of being unfairly expected to know everything or to learn it the first time.

Examples

The use of examples is a valuable device in teaching. The importance of a nearly equal swimming pace, for example, can be emphasized by the story of the race between the tortoise and the hare. The rapid bursts of speed of the rabbit followed by distracting activities, were overcome by the steady, unbroken, speed or pace of the turtle. But if the children being instructed have not heard the story, or don't know what a tortoise or a hare are, then the example is lost.

Coaches must remember that their particular experiences and age often put them in a different world and examples from their own experience mean nothing to the children. Examples drawn from movies, TV shows, and songs the children know will often work well because they capture and hold the children's attention.

Non-verbal communication

We communicate our ideas and feelings as much by gestures, movements, and facial expressions, as with words. Coaches are often not aware of how much of this nonverbal communication they do.

When a swimmer looks for consent or approval, the coach may nod and smile or frown and shake his head. We hold out our hands in front, palms up, to indicate either impatience, futility, or to ask for help or suggestions.

If the coach walks in whistling and happy or frowning and looking depressed, the coach has already communicated a good deal to the swimmers before a word is said. Non-verbal communication is essential if one is to be effective. The danger comes when un-intended messages or contradictory messages are sent non-verbally.

For example, when talking to some swimmers, the coach always smiles, is pleasant, pats them on the back, nods, and generally shows many signs that he likes and accepts them. Talking to others, the coach may **say** things like, "Yes, I'll consider you for the relay team, and your chances are pretty good." But while saying this, if non-verbal behavior is a frown, a slow shaking of the head, hands behind the back with the hands only appearing to reach out palms up, while he shrugs, the verbal message is contradicted by clear non-verbal signs that there is little chance of this swimmer being on the relay team.

Disagreement between verbal and non-verbal messages often leads to swimmers or parents saying that they don't like or trust a coach. Disagreement between verbal and non-verbal messages is taken by most people as evidence that a person is insincere and untrustworthy.

There is good reason for this because there is much evidence that people who send such contradictory messages are themselves likely to be confused or insincere.

Equally important, research has shown clearly that when people send one message verbally, in what they say, and a conflicting message non-verbally, in their facial expressions and gestures, it is the **non-verbal** message that observers are most likely to believe. The message they receive from the eyes, where much expression can be shown, from posture, and gestures, speaks louder than words.

Direct and indirect behavior

Communication is a two-way process back and forth between coach and team members and between team members. The coach has authority. If not careful, that authority can be used to dominate the situation so fully that communication is only one way. It is certainly necessary that the coach uses authority to establish necessary order and control and to get and keep swimmers working in what was referred to earlier as a business-like or formal way.

Direct control by the coach is achieved by giving instructions, giving information about technique, criticizing performance or behavior, and giving corrections. Direct coaching behavior focuses on the task, the business, at hand.

It is important that the coach develops skill in "being human" and acting more indirectly. The coach should accept honest ideas and questions from swimmers, give them encouragement and help them clear up errors and misconceptions in a friendly unthreatening way. The use of humour should be non-threatening, joining in their fun, making jokes they can enjoy together, and never be used against individuals. It humiliates children and adults alike.

The ability to be firm, direct, in control, when necessary, and to swing over to a more relaxed, informal, indirect style of communication is described as a flexible coaching style. It is not always easy to achieve but the benefits of being able to do it are so great that it is well worth working on.

Respect

A good guideline for coaches to use is to adopt two simple rules described by Haim Ginott in his paperback book, **Between Parent and Child**. The first is that all communication spoken and unspoken, be designed to preserve the self-respect of both the coach and swimmer. This means that name-calling, ranting and raving, unfounded accusations are out. They often challenge the self-respect of both coach and swimmers.

The second rule Ginott suggests is that the coach should listen carefully and be sure he understands fully what the swimmer wants to say in a situation where some problem has developed or is developing. Only after he is sure that he understands how the swimmer sees the situation should be offer advice or information or take corrective action. If the coach "jumps" into a potential problem, making swift and hard decisions, he may find that he has painted himself into a corner from which it is difficult to escape.

Ginott also suggests that advice or instruction offered, after **hearing out** the swimmers involved in a problem, begin with some statements of empathy or understanding by the coach. There is an important distinction between statements of understanding and statements of agreement. One can understand or have empathy for another without agreeing that they are right.

For example, if two boys have skipped an important workout, the coach should just talk it over to find out exactly why they did so. It may turn out that they just didn't want to attend. But it may be that one didn't attend because of being very upset with something that heppened at home or school. His friend may have joined him to give him some support. Once the coach knows exactly what happened, he might say, "I can understand how you felt. I've felt that way myself. But remember that you knew we were going to have time trials today on which to base our entries for our next meet." Then, depending on the circumstances, he may have to take the hard line and not enter the boys or he may decide to give them another chance if their past record warrants it.

In either case a major blowup may be avoided and future relationships still have a chance of working. Of course, if similar incidents occur frequently, the situation may require a suspension. But, even if that happens, it does not have to become an all-out personal war that no one wins and that upsets everybody. Furthermore, hard feelings can spread beyond the people immediately concerned and erode the morale of the entire team.

Feelings are contagious

Another important communication principle is that feelings are contagious. We have no trouble being polite to those who are polite to us. We show respect to those who respect us. We can be hostile with no effort at all to those who are hostile to us.

Some children receive little sensible guidance in their home lives. Others experience disrespect and bad treatment quite regularly. In either case they know very little about how to show respect and consideration to others. These children need to be told firmly what type of behavior is not allowed in the team. But, equally important, they need to clearly **told** and **shown** how to behave with respect and consideration. They also need a little more patience from the coach while they are learning these things than do well controlled children. If this is done, most unruly, unreliable children will begin to improve and mature in their relations with others. However, there will be no miracles.

Punish the deed

A helpful approach to improving communications and relations with so-called problem children is to be careful to punish the deed rather than the child. Note the difference between punishing the deed and the child. Perhaps a boy has been rudely interrupting the coach while he is explaining a drill and gentle attempts to stop him have failed. The coach might say, "John, that is an inconsiderate thing to do. Your behavior is preventing twenty of your teammates from learning this. Please be quiet and pay attention or I will have to ask you to go." It is the deed that is the focus of attention. The coach's remarks preserve both his own respect and that of the boy.

Contrast that with this alternative action by the coach, "John you are a nuisance. You are always causing trouble. Why don't you shut up or get lost!" This approach not only attacks the self-respect of the boy but shows the coach to be immature. It would likely upset many of the innocent bystanders as well as the coach and the boy.

Effective communication is worth constant attention. It can never be perfected but one can continue to grow in ability to communicate if one tries. Such improvement will not only make coaching more satisfying and effective but it will carry over into other aspects of the coach's life.

2 TEACHING—COACHING TECHNIQUES

Dr. Murray Smith,
Professor of Physical Education,
University of Alberta, Edmonton

TEACHING — COACHING TECHNIQUES

INTRODUCING NEW STROKES AND SKILLS

The coach is responsible for directing swimmers in the learning of techniques. These include the four competitive styles and individual medley. The racing techniques; starting, turning and finishing, as they apply to the various events, are also part of the coach's teaching responsibilities.

There are many methods for teaching swimming techniques. The effectiveness of a method is the result obtained by its use. Coaches should judge the effectiveness of a method through personal observation and by trying to obtain honest reaction from the swimmer under instruction.

THE USE OF EFFECTIVE METHODS

Sometimes coaches are tempted to blame the swimmers for being slow to learn instead of realizing that the method could be improved. While it is true that many different methods can be made to work, it is also true that some methods are much more effective with more swimmers than other methods.

We will discuss teaching the strokes and then the other important competitive skills.

Be prepared to refer to the sections on techniques in the Level One manual: "An Introduction to Swimming Coaching", by Cecil Colwin.

CONSTANT REPETITION — AN IMPORTANT PART OF THE LEARNING PROCESS

When coaching young swimmers just starting in competitive swimming, the following rule is important: Be tolerant of errors in stroke technique until the swimmer can complete at least two hundred meters non-stop. The swimmer then will have sufficient endurance to enable practice to occur. Eventually, the swimmer will be able to repeat many movements in correcting errors and establishing desired stroke-patterns. Developing the necessary endurance to spend adequate time in practising will avoid frustration and discouragement. Remember: "repetition, repetition, repetition" is an important part of the learning process. The more times a movement is repeated the more habitual and automatic it becomes.

DEMONSTRATE, EXPLAIN SIMPLY, AND PRACTISE: STROKES

A simple workable method to introduce a new stroke is to have a fairly good swimmer demonstrate

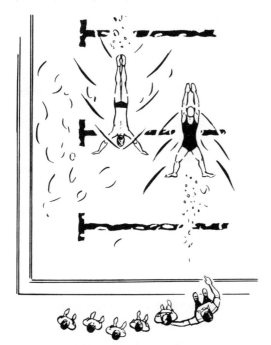

Front and rear views

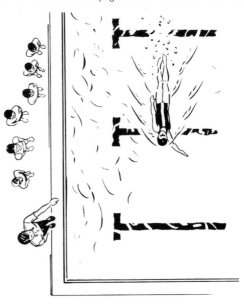

Side View

USING PUPILS TO DEMONSTRATE

by swimming across the pool while the coach gives the class a simple explanation. It is best to use a swimmer of about the same age as those being taught. This helps learners identify with the demonstrator. It is also better if the demonstrator is not too far above the skill level of those being taught. The time for the near-perfect demonstration is after learners have a good feel for the stroke.

By having the demonstrator swim across the pool, observers can see well without having to move. The demonstrator should swim slowly across the pool three or four times, stopping after each width to allow brief comment by the coach. Then the demonstrator should swim directly towards the learners and directly away from them. This should be repeated several times. This procedure will give the class good front and rear views.

There should not be a long explanation before the demonstration starts. Start the demonstration at once. Focus attention on only one or two parts of the style.

A sensible order is to focus attention first on body position, then on arm-action, then the kick, then breathing pattern, and finally the coordination of the complete style.

DON'T TELL THEM EVERYTHING YOU KNOW!

Perhaps the most common fault, even among experienced coaches, is to try to explain everything they know about a particular topic. For example, when introducing a style, do not include an explanation of differences between sprint and distance styles. Leave these and other details until later. The coach should allow concepts of desired movements to develop gradually in the swimmers' minds. Explaining too much too soon after results in "mental indigestion". If questions of small detail are asked, receive them with respect and either answer them quickly or say that this will be discussed and explained in the near future. (The coach should ensure that the promise **is** kept at a later date.)

When the demonstration is completed, the swimmers should be put to work at once with some clear focus to their attention. A good way to do this is for them to swim lengths in waves of swimmers equal in number to the number of lanes in the pool. Six swimmers abreast in six lane pools, eight abreast in eight lanes, etc.

Instructions for the first two lengths of freestyle might be: "Push off, stretch, pause and feel how your body is stretched and streamlined. Then swim at

moderate speed with a good reach in front at the entry of each arm. Think about keeping your shoulders square to the lane line under you (your line of motion), don't overreach."

Swimmers should stop at the end of each length. Give a brief reminder before they swim each length.

The next instruction might be: "Push off, stretch, remember try to be aware of keeping your shoulders square at each hand entry. Now try to think about keeping your elbow up as you start the pull, feel the pressure of the water as your hand pulls, then push well back below your waist." It will help if the coach demonstrates the desired movement while giving the instruction.

DEMONSTRATE, EXPLAIN AND THEN HAVE THEM PRACTISE

Attention may now be directed to the kick and breathing, and finally to coordination. The first time a style is introduced in a season, demonstration, explanation and practice lengths should be included in a time-frame of up to thirty minutes. The second time in the season this is featured in a workout, the work may be reviewed and practised as described above, in fifteen to twenty minutes. The third and fourth times, the review might be completed in five to ten minutes. During each review, one or two new refinements or details should be added and the attention of the swimmers focused on these during practice lengths.

It is sound policy to review all strokes, starts, turns, and changes, early each season, requiring all swimmers, regardless of experience, to repeat this review process. This is the time the coach can explain desired changes in technique and make the necessary refinements.

Before starting to build early-season mileage, the coach should first ensure that the swimmers' technique-patterns have been established. These include not only the actual swimming styles but also starts, turns and race-finishing techniques.

TEACH ARM-ACTION FIRST FOR GREATER MOVEMENT CONTROL

First work on developing the arm-action in the style. Most coaches and reference books begin by working on the leg action and later, the arm action. You might want to try both these approaches yourself. There is strong reason to believe that developing the arm-action first, in most instances, may produce skilled swimming in a shorter time. Firstly, the arm-action has a profound effect on body-balance. If the arm-action is skilled, head mechanics, body-position and leg-action become easier to integrate with the complete style. Furthermore, the hands have great dexterity and are more capable of skilled action of any kind. The arm-movements occur, for the most part, within the normal field of vision and are thus more easily controlled. Because the arms provide most of the propulsion, the swimmer often has a greater sense of achievement by learning the arm-action first.

USING DRILLS FOR CORRECT DETAIL OF STROKES

Teach general movements first. Complex actions come later.

The Level One textbook describes very useful drills for developing correct stroke technique. Once the swimmers have a good general technique for each stroke, work should begin on developing detailed technique. Do not be fussy about details until swimmers have a fair idea of the stroke, and can perform it reasonably well.

It is much the same as the young child first learning to print. If the teacher insists that all letters printed by the child must be near-perfect from the beginning, there will be unnecessary tension and frustration for both pupil and teacher. Motivation and keenness will be hampered, to say nothing of enjoyment.

It is necessary to accept the fact that the ability to perform complex acts such as the competitive strokes and skills, develop slowly, emerge gradually from early crude attempts to the later highly skilled performance of the mature athlete.

BE TOLERANT OF ERRORS

A willingness to be more tolerant of errors during early stages of learning will amost surely improve final results. One need only think of the way in which piano lessons were often taught in the past. Correct hand and finger position were required from the very beginning. Scales and exercises were all that were played. Even when the first selections were attempted, they were those the teacher thought should be played. Enjoyment and success were not experienced by many pupils. The results were very often the reverse of intentions. Many children quit lessons and convinced their parents, by fair means or foul, that it was a lost cause.

Children change and grow and there is much to

be said for taking a reasonable and moderate approach in our demands especially during the early introduction to competitive swimming. As talent is revealed and performances improve, there should be an increase in demand for discipline and correct technique in minute detail.

When the swimmer has a good idea of how the main features of a style or skill should be done, then introduce more detail into the stroke-action to improve the accuracy and refinement of the movement.

DEVELOP ENDURANCE SO THAT BEGINNERS ARE ABLE TO PRACTISE SUFFICIENT MOVEMENT REPETITIONS

It is worth repeating that swimmers should be able to swim at least two hundred meters non-stop before attention is given to detailed stroke correction. Before that time, the efforts of the coach will be better spent encouraging swimmers to improve their endurance. During this stage, the coach should make only general corrections. Coaches know that some swimmers correct many of their own mistakes, but by no means all of them, as they improve their endurance. Endurance swims also develop an innate sense of rhythm. Five to ten minutes should be set aside for regular practice of stroke-accuracy drills, once the swimmer has reached this stage of development.

COMMUNICATION

For example, in using Drill One from page 47 of the Level One Manual ("Introduction to Swimming Coaching" — Level One Manual, p. 47), arrange swimmers on the end of the pool and have a demonstrator swim across the pool as described and illustrated on page 47. Use plain language to explain the purpose of the drill; **why** it is important. Use plain language to explain **how** it is done. Focus attention on the demonstrator. Ask for any questions and be careful to receive them with respect. Never ridicule any question or questioner or allow others to do so. This will be discussed in more detail in a later section.

Then have swimmers perform the drill and look first for what is being done either correctly or quite well. Then look for any fairly common errors. At first have the swimmers stop every length or two for a brief comment. Begin by pointing out the things that are being fairly well done and then, as simply as possible, identify the one or two (no more) common errors and explain how to correct them. For example: "You are all getting the feel of it quite well. You are turning smoothly from side to side. This time, check to see if the corners of your eye and mouth are just touching the surface. Be careful to avoid kicking too wide!"

Repeat this pattern of encouragement and further correction several times. Then begin to check individuals and work with them to improve performance.

DEMONSTRATE, EXPLAIN SIMPLY, AND PRACTISE: SKILLS

The starts, turns, individual medley turns, relay changes, and the techniques of finishing a race are the skills of competitive swimming.

These skills should be taught by methods similar to those described for the strokes. Begin with a simple demonstration of the skill. Use the drills contained in the Level One Manual. Allow a fixed amount of time, say fifteen to to twenty minutes for introducing and practising a new skill. Don't spend too long a time on a new skill. Regular, shorter periods of practice will provide better results than a few long periods. Spending fifteen minutes on the freestyle turn in each of six practices, a total of ninety minutes, will produce more improvement than two periods of forty-five minutes or three periods of thirty minutes.

REVISE AND CONSOLIDATE BUT ALSO WORK FOR GRADUAL PROGRESSION

Again, do not be too demanding at the beginning. Be willing to accept a general idea of the skill as a good starting point. As workouts progress, the coach should require a higher and higher standard. Don't forget to revise and consolidate what has been taught in previous sessions. Because new and complex skills cannot be mastered at once, patience and tolerance at this stage will pay off.

It is beneficial to pair off a beginning swimmer with a more experienced swimmer who can perform the skill well. Swimmers do a great deal of learning from each other and often help each other over difficulties.

It is important that the beginner be paired with someone they like and trust. A good way to ensure this is to ask newcomers to provide a list of the three or four experienced swimmers they would most like to have help them. Then good pairings can be made. The coach's own judgement will also help. Pair off a shy, hesitant newcomer with a considerate, helpful swimmer. Put a noisy, difficult to handle newcomer with a firm, confident, leader-type. Such pairings can also be valuable in improving strokes.

Every couple of months, swimmers should be asked to give a list of those they would best like to work with. Both experienced and inexperienced swimmers should indicate their choices. The coach may not be able to satisfy everyone with their first choice but perhaps every swimmer might get no worse than second or third choice. This procedure very effectively can multiply the efforts of the coach and generate much valuable team spirit.

"Pair off a beginner with someone more experienced. Swimmers often help each other and do a great deal of learning from each other."

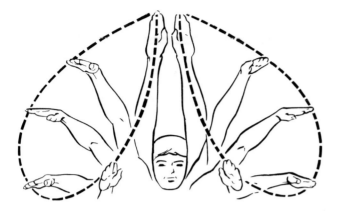

1. MOVING VIEWPOINT (BREASTSTROKE)
("arms-past-the-torso")

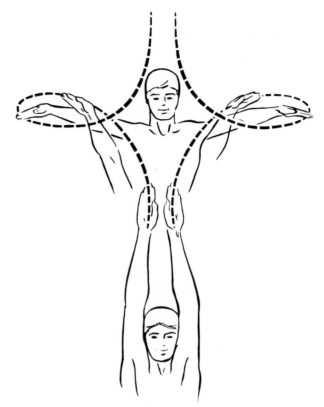

2. FIXED VIEWPOINT (BREASTSTROKE)
("torso-past-the-arms")

For all intents and purposes, the swimmer is in water that is stationary. Although there may be minor turbulences, each part of the body moves through still water. It is important for the coach to consistently keep this fixed point of view in mind, for only then can one fully appreciate the fluid forces involved in swimming. But the moving point of view has validity as well because it is the way a swimmer sees what he/she is doing; the coach's dryland demonstrations, therefore, can be very meaningful for the swimmer. In short, the coach should use the fixed point of view when assessing a swimmer's movements and then switch to the moving point of view when suggesting improvements.

OTHER VIEWING CONSIDERATIONS

Normally the coach has a clear, undistorted view of only those parts of the swimmer's body that are above the surface. Refraction drastically reshapes and diminishes or magnifies the actual movements of submerged body parts when viewing from the pool deck. For example, flutterkicking seen from six lanes away will appear much narrower and shallower than it actually is. And of course waves and froth and foam further distort or even obliterate the view. **There is no escaping the fact that the worst angles of view are from the pool deck; knowing this, many experienced coaches make it a regular practice to observe their swimmers from a diving tower or board, an elevated guard chair, or even a starting block.**

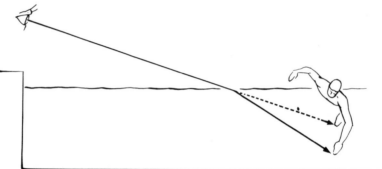

"Refraction of light reshapes, diminishes or magnifies movements of submerged body parts...when viewed from the pool deck."

It goes without saying that the coach can learn to compensate for the distortion that is seen, but really, the only adequate solution is for the coach to view the swimmers from below the surface. The simplest way is for the coach to don goggles or a facemask and go below, perhaps assisted by scuba or skin-diving equipment. Underwater windows are good, especially when there is a microphone jack near the window so the coach can speak to the swimmer through the P.A. system. And of course movies or video-taped shots from below are an asset, although they are not the panacea some might suppose; gadgets cannot replace the expressive coach/demonstrator.

For large groups, the **buddy-coach system** works well. The coach, in effect, borrows the eyes of the swimmers who pair off and take turns observing and criticizing some **specified** aspect of each other's underwater movements. One swimmer swims two widths while the other, wearing goggles, ducks below the surface and watches a partner. (Widths permit more coaching stations.) The observer then tells the buddy the good and/or bad features of what was seen. First, of course, the coach explains to the group the right and the wrong of the **specific** aspect of the stroke — bent-arm pull, or whatever — they are to concentrate on. While the buddy-coaching is going on the coach may move from pair to pair reinforcing their findings and "repairs". A bonus is that the swimmers also gain from the act of observing and criticizing.

PROPULSION

Simply stated, propulsion is the force that moves the swimmer forward as he swims. Until quite recently, most coaching authorities had it that propulsion is the result of the drag force that the hands and feet and arms and legs create as they push backward. It was presumed, for example, that the swimmer merely "anchored" a hand and forearm in the water and exerted force rearward. Now, however, propulsion in swimming is better understood. To be sure, an appreciable amount of propulsion results from the sea-anchor/kedging effect just described, but the best swimmers have, all along, employed a rather different phenomenon to achieve propulsion. They do not pull-push directly rearward (as they would if they were using a simple action-reaction, oar-like form of propulsion); instead, the track of the hand when observed from the moving point of view (discussed earlier) resembles a letter "S" or a question mark "?". They make use of an age-old alternate way of effectively using a paddle: they scull their hands through a zig-zag pattern.

To fully understand this using of the hands as sculling blades there are several principles of fluid mechanics that must be reviewed.

BERNOULLI'S PRINCIPLE

This principle or law states that when a fluid moves relative to a surface the pressure of the fluid against that surface is reduced when the speed of flow is increased.

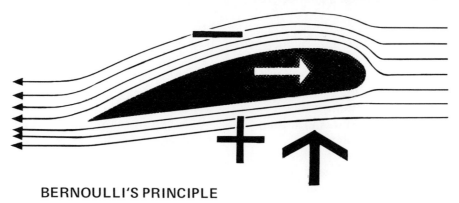

BERNOULLI'S PRINCIPLE

The propeller blade and the airplane wing are designed to make use of this principle, not to mention "Nature's handiwork" in shaping the flippers and flukes (tail planes) of the dolphin and other similar creatures. Their cross-sectional shape (foil) and their angles to their direction of motion (pitch) are, or can be, such that the fluid forced over the front or upper surfaces must move farther, and therefore faster, than the fluid passing over the back or under surface. When the foil shape and pitch are right, great differences in pressure are created and the blade or wing is thrust forcefully toward the zone of lower pressure.

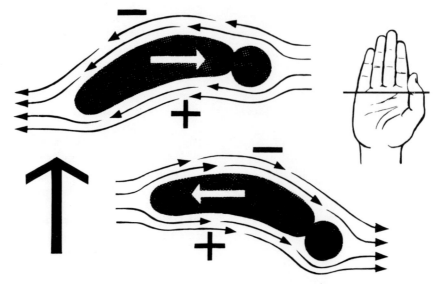

CROSS-SECTIONAL VIEWS OF SCULLING HAND

In the same way, the hand of a swimmer, when it is held at the proper angle relative to its path through the water, can serve as a lift-producing foil or propeller blade to provide forward propulsion to the swimmer.

Greater propulsion in water is obtained by moving a large amount of water a short distance than by moving a small amount a great distance. The propeller of a boat, when delivering thrust, never relies on pushing water backward; **it moves forward in still water**. With every turn it operates in new, stationary water, never, itself, moving backward. This type of action also occurs through the so-called arm-pulls of the best swimmers, giving them an advantage. If a swimmer pull-pushes the hand in a straight-line pattern, one is pushing a little water a long way with great acceleration. Once the water around the hand has been started backward by the movement of the arm, the swimmer obtains less and less traction or propulsion, and soon virtually none at all, from this backward-moving water. So the wise swimmer, the well-coached swimmer, moves the hand in an elliptical pattern in order to continue encountering still water; the swimmer "works" one piece of water, then moves the hand sideways to the next piece, and so on. In short, the swimmer uses a sculling action.

Other considerations, when comparing the merits of sculling versus straight-line pulling, are as follows: When a hand applies pressure, hoe-like, directly backward in a straight-line pattern, the drag it depends on for traction squares with the speed of the pulling hand. This would seem at first fortuitous, a phenomenon to

be exploited...triple the speed of the hand, enjoy nine times the drag/propulsion. But there is a catch: The physiological cost, in terms of muscle effort expended, does not square, it cubes! **The straight-line puller must pay exhorbitantly for any increase in swimming speed.** and is therefore unlikely to succeed in endurance events, if succeeding at all.

Of course the sculling-hand action "costs", too, when speeded up but, because of its more streamlined shape, it experiences a minimal amount of drag, a small fraction in fact, in comparison with the straight-line method; the squaring/cubing problem is hardly a factor.

Thus far, we have discussed only the use of the hands in propulsion. The forearms, and to a lesser extent the upper arms also figure in the total front-end propulsion packet. The wrist and the lower part of the forearm are also reasonably well shaped for sculling. The truth is that the best swimmers derive propulsion from the arm and hand through a combination of drag-traction and sculling. Considerable propulsion is possible when the hands are closed into fists. The sculling-blading of the hands is an **extra factor** that helps set championship-class swimmers apart from their run-of-the-mill teammates; it can make the difference between merely qualifying to enter the meet and getting into the finals, and winning.

HAND SHAPE

How best to hold one's hand for maximum propulsion from sculling?, from drag-traction? For both uses of the hand the answer is the same: hand flat, with fingers and thumb together. The worst shapes are: hands cupped; and hand flat but at an angle.

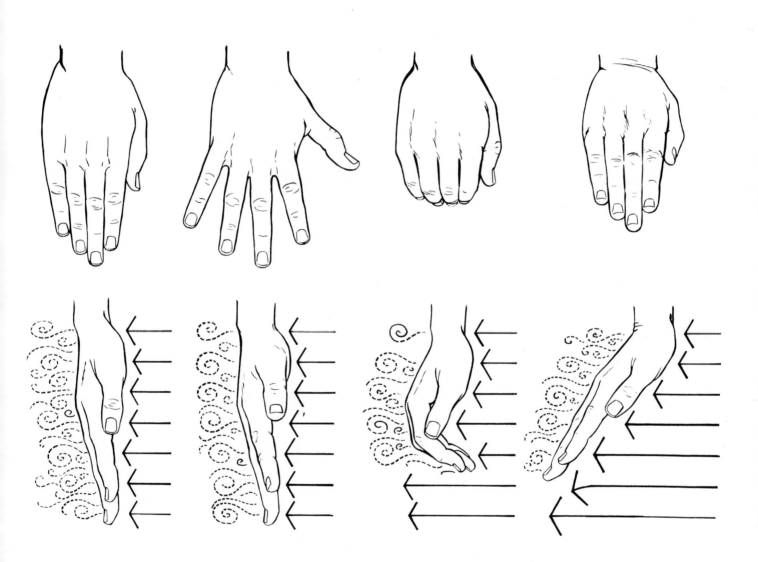

THE LEGS ARE PROPELLING UNITS

Freestyle

Very little, if any, useful propulsion is derived from the kick in freestyle. In this stroke the arms haul the legs along faster than they can propel themselves. (If in some way the swimmer could be safely severed through the waist, the hips and legs would be left behind.)

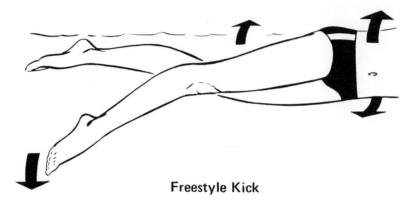

Freestyle Kick

So why is a freestyler faster when kicking? The swimmer is faster because the legs serve quite another purpose than propelling: They aid in steering and tipping the swimmer from side to side about the longitudinal axis in time with the swimmer's stroking so one can split through the water, javelin-like, with greatly-reduced resistance.

The six-beat flutter kick is the classic it is because six divides into odd numbers: three and three. This permits a ONE-two-three/ONE-two-three rhythm with the slightly accented ONE's coming in time with the shifting from side to side. The two-beat kick, the broken-tempo kick, and even the so-called cross-over kick all serve this purpose when used by the best swimmers.

The legs can perform their role as "body-rotators" best when their kicking emanates from the hips, with only slight flexions of the knees and with the feet pointed. Happily, when performing this action, the legs add their tapered length, improving the swimmer's streamlining (better laminar flow).

Backstroke

The stroke demands a steady and powerful "leg-drive". As in freestyle, and for the same reason, six kicks per stroke cycle is the norm, in fact virtually all world-class backstrokers use the six-beat kicking rhythm.

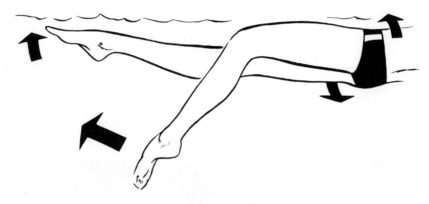

Backstroke Kick

However, in backstroke, the knees flex more, sending the feet deeper than in freestyle in order to obtain more rearward drag-traction-type propulsion. The knees, themselves, move up and down very little (pumping the knees out of water is a serious fault). The feet contribute more thrust when they are allowed to fall inward, pidgeon-toed, thus flattening and increasing the area of the upper surfaces of the feet as the legs straighten with each kick.

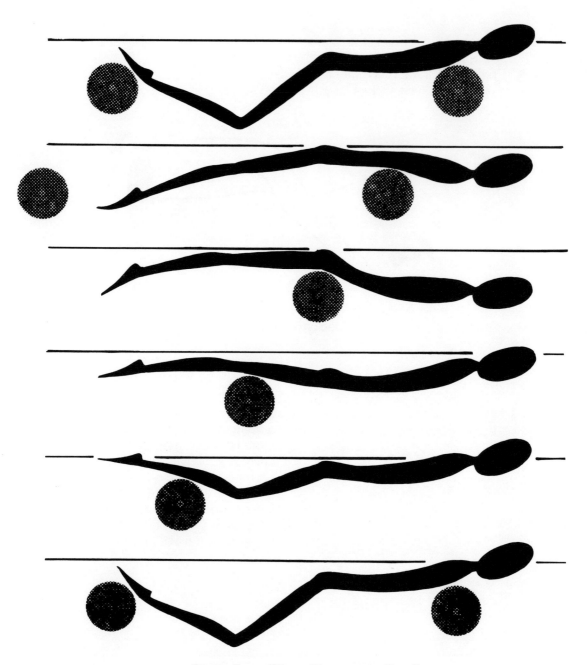

Butterfly — "Travelling wave effect"

Butterfly

Strictly speaking, the kick in butterfly is more than just a leg action. The torso with its flexible spine and even the head contribute to the eel-like "travelling wave effect" that originates at the base of the skull and culminates with each whip-cracking snap of the feet. When practising the kick even the kickboard should "get into the act" and bounce along.

EXERCISE FOUR

starting position   support

1.

2.

3.

4.

5.

6.

EXERCISE FIVE

support

1.

2.

3.

4.

The leg is straightened to the side and held about 12 inches from the floor (1). It is then turned inward with the knee bent and thigh across the body (2). The thigh is then lifted as high as possible (3), turned sideways (4) where the leg is again straightened and locked (5). At this point the leg moves in a circular movement four times (6).

Note:—This is done 4 times **without** putting the foot back on the ground. THEN the starting position is resumed. The exercise should be done slowly. Repeat using the other leg.

BALLET EXERCISES FOR SWIMMERS

Both heels are raised from the ground (1). With the body kept erect, go to the squat position (2). The leg furthest from the support is then extended slowly until straight (3). At this point, using the support leg **only**, the body is brought to an upright position with the leg still extended in front (4). This should be repeated four times on each leg.

Note:—**Care should be taken with this exercise since it can cause leg strain.**

BALLET EXERCISES FOR SWIMMERS

EXERCISE SIX

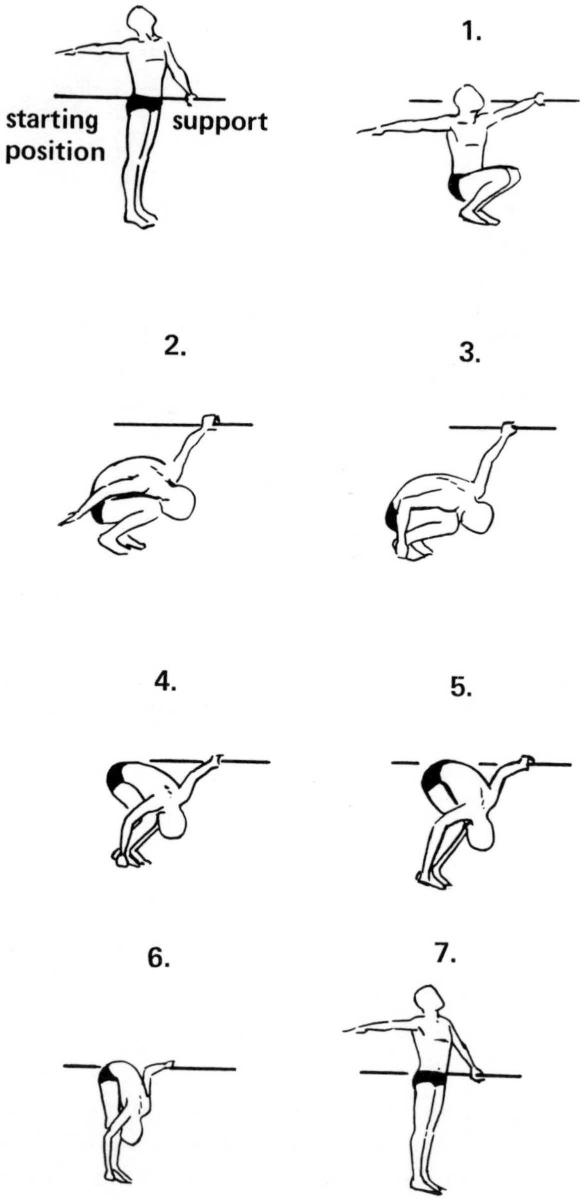

starting position   support

1.

2.   **3.**

4.   **5.**

6.   **7.**

In the starting position, the body is erect and the right arm is held horizontally. The heels are raised and the legs bent to the squat position with the back erect (1). The head is then placed on the knees (2) and the heel is grasped with the free hand (3). The knees are slowly straightened without the head being lifted from them (4, 5 and 6). Recovery to the starting position is then carried out (7). This exercise should be executed 6 to 8 times very slowly on each side.

BALLET EXERCISES FOR SWIMMERS

ORGANIZING THE FLEXIBILITY PROGRAM

Just as it is important to have some group organization for ensuring maximum effectiveness of a weight program (see Chapter 6), it is important to have a group structure that will ensure that each swimmer in the club is benefiting from the flexibility program.

Unlike the weight program, flexibility does not lend itself to the circuit system of organization. The aim of the flexibility routine is not to increase muscular strength, although, as already shown, strength may be a by-product of some systems of flexibility exercises. The aim of flexibility exercise is to increase the range of movement about the body joints and facilitate muscle relaxation.

There are two ways to approach the flexibility session. **One, is to allow the swimmers to work either alone or with a partner and go through a series of flexibility exercises at their own pace, selecting exercises as they themselves see fit.** The advantages in this approach to the flexibility session are:

a) The swimmers themselves may work on the areas of their own musculature which tend to lack mobility and need to have a greater range of movement. Not everyone lacks mobility in the same areas.

b) Swimmers can be "stroke-specific" with their flexibility work. For example, breaststroke swimmers may work as they please on leg positions required for good breaststroke. There are other similar specific areas of the body which require specialized attention if the other swimming styles are to be well-performed.

c) This system allows the swimmers to be innovative. That is, swimmers can develop exercises themselves to stretch areas not commonly dealt with in tests on flexibility. Some of the shoulder and back muscles, in particular, fall into this category.

d) The swimmers can work at their own rate.

A second approach to the flexibility program is through the "follow the leader" system. Somebody from the group, (who needs not necessarily be a good model) is selected to lead the group through a series of flexibility exercises going from one exercise to the other as the person sees fit.

Since the model is a peer to the other members of the group, there is usually a healthy group tone prevailing in the session. The scope of the session is increased dramatically.

The flexibility program can be designed to move slowly from one exercise to another with individual leader preferences emphasized or be made into a smooth rhythmical routine set to music of general appeal. This latter form of stretching actually becomes a mild form of workout incorporating within it a system of stretching known as "fast" or "bounce" stretching. **However, this form of exercise usually leaves an aftermath of muscle soreness. It also carries with it the risk of muscle tears. For this reason, this method of flexibility work is only mentioned here briefly. It will not be part of this chapter but will be dealt with in the level III Manual.**

There is a certain amount of innovation required on the part of the leader to see that the routine flows smoothly and that all major muscle groups have been covered. This type of flexibility organization would most likely be the one a coach would use in the working phase of the swim program; since, as mentioned earlier, a workload can be integrated into the program.

In each of the above approaches to organizing a flexibility period for club training, it should be noted that the coach is free to move among the swimmers offering suggestions, guidance and correction where necessary. For this reason alone, these methods are far superior to a situation where the coach calls the teacher and the group carries it out. That is, the coach is tied to the "role of instructing".

HOW OFTEN SHOULD STRETCHING BE DONE?

On the question of the frequency of flexibility exercises, there is no correct answer except to say, **weight work should always be followed by a flexibility session,** and **stretching should always precede workouts and any competition.**

Therefore, it can be seen that, in the normal working week of the swim club, there might be as many as 11 - 14 flexibility periods allocated. The flexibility sessions need only last about 10 - 15 minutes in order to be effective. The important point is that, as with most things, a number of short, regular flexibility sessions spread over the training week of the club are better than one or two prolonged sessions.

This approach appears to be suggested by research on flexibility which shows increases in the range of limb movements through flexibility lasts for relatively short periods. **Therefore, to be of use, flexibility exercises should be done regularly!**

An important distinction should be made at this juncture...the distinction between "flexibility" exercises and "limbering up" exercises. While the difference is quite clear to many, there are even more who confuse the two. **Flexibility exercise is exercise aimed at increasing the range of movement possible in a given joint.** This is attained by systematically working with exercises based on the procedures already outlined. The "limbering up" process includes arm swinging, arm jiggling, leg jiggling, hand shaking, ankle shaking and such activities a swimmer might participate in to ensure complete muscle relaxation in these areas. These are usually pre-race actions but they can be used anywhere. **Limbering up routines do not stretch muscle groups.**

A weight program, followed by a stretching routine, followed by a limbering up process is a good habit to establish with swimmers before they enter the water for a workout. Similarly, stretching routines, followed by the limbering process, is a good pre-race habit to establish in club swimmers.

SUMMARY

This chapter has emphasized that swimmers should have a wide range of movement about the joints if they are:
1) to easily attain the stroke positions necessary in each of the swimming styles;
2) to enjoy maximum muscle relaxation; and
3) maximize metabolism in the muscle, joints and associated connective tissues.

To this end, three systems of flexibility exercise were discussed. The first system, scientific stretching for sport **(3S)**, enables swimmers to work in pairs and use their own initiative to stretch various muscle groups. Because this method involves isometric contractions, strength gains in the swimmer are evident.

The second system of flexibility exercise **(SS system of stretching)** is appropriate to the club situation. These slow-stretch exercises can be done mostly by the swimmer working alone. They also provide opportunity for the swimmer to be inventive in designing exercises to stretch certain muscle groups.

A third system of flexibility exercise which was discussed was **ballet exercises for swimmers**. It was pointed out that this type of flexibility is more applicable to breaststroke swimmers. Strength increases, in the legs and ankles, are additional benefits of this form of mobility exercise.

Two organizational methods for conducting flexibility periods were discussed. One allowed the swimmers to work at their own pace doing what exercises they wished to do. The other was a "follow the leader" group organization. Both methods have

the advantage of allowing the coach to move freely about the group offering suggestions and corrections where necessary.

Finally, suggestions were made on how frequently stretching routines should be carried out at the club level. In this respect it was advised that they should be done following **all** weight workouts, before training sessions in the water and before competition.

Reference was made on the difference between flexibility exercises and limbering up activities as these are sometimes thought of as being synonymous with each other when in fact, they are not. The practice of weight work, followed by flexibility work, followed by limbering up, followed by water work, was mentioned as being a good practice for swimmers to follow. Similarly, **"flexibility, limber up, compete"** was proposed as being a routine suitable for all competition situations.

REFERENCES

Hardie, A. Ballet Exercises for Athletes. Royal Academy of Dancing, London.

Holt, L.E. Scientific Stretching for Sport. Dalhousie University, Halifax, Nova Scotia, 1976.

Howell, M.L., Morton, W.R. Fitness Training Methods. C.A.P.H.E.R. Toronto, 1966.

Kiphuth, R.J.H. Swimming. Nicholas Kaye, London, 1949.

Scholz, A.E., Johnson, R.E. Body, Conditioning for Men. W.B. Saunders, Toronto, 1969.

Turner, A.A. The effects of two training methods on flexibility. M.Sc. Thesis. Lakehead University, 1977.

Widdop, J.H. Effects of ballet training program upon the physical performance of college freshman. Research Quarterly, October, 1968. 39:3.

6 WEIGHT TRAINING

Mr. Don Talbot, Head Swimming Coach,
Thunder Bay Thunderbolts,
Thunder Bay, Ontario

WEIGHT TRAINING FOR EXTRA POWER IN SWIMMING

THE CLUB PROGRAM

THE WEIGHT TRAINING CONTROVERSY IN SWIMMING

Opinions differ concerning the use of weights by swimmers to improve their power in the water. Research seems to indicate that weight programs contribute little to the development of speed in swimming. At least, evidence shows that this is true at the elite levels where mature competitors are involved.

However, practical experience shows that swimmers who have worked with weights for years do derive benefit from weight training. In fact, there is enough anecdotal evidence to claim that a club program should include weight training to be successful.

Why there might be a difference between research and what happens in actual practice will be discussed in level III of the certification program. It seems reasonable at this stage to state that weight work does help the swimmer...although under what conditions this occurs is not altogether clear. **Until definitive statements can be made to clarify the question, the wise coach will provide weight training in the club program.**

EQUIPMENT

Since commercially-manufactured weight equipment is expensive, the coach is well advised to consider carefully the approach he/she will take to improving the swimmers' strength and power **before** deciding what items of equipment to purchase.

Basically, there are three common methods in use in club weight programs. One system involves the use of relatively light weights with high repetitions. The next incorporates heavy weights with a low number of repetitions.

Equipping for either of these programs can be costly.

Finally, there are some coaches who, at various times in their swimming calendar, use one system and, at other times, use the other system.

The decision by the coach, using this approach, whether to use heavy or light weights is based on factors such as the swimmers' experience, their ages, their sex and where the team is in its preparation; the importance of the next competition, etc. Coaches, using this latter concept, also will often use a **combination** of light and heavy weights in one workout.

The commercial market is glutted with weight equipment said to be endowed with "magic" properties designed to provide "more" than the equipment designed by rival companies. Actually, a well-designed program can be set up with almost **any** equipment! In fact, many coaches have resorted to making their own equipment!

The concept of "more expensive being best" does not necessarily apply in the case of weight equipment. There is no conclusive evidence at this time, either from research or practice, to indicate that a strength-training machine designed on the principles of iso-kinetics, isometrics or any other principles of weight training, is any better than exercise done with the olympic bar, which has been the mainstay of strength equipment in gymnasiums throughout the world for decades.

In fact, any sort of weight program based on any system will improve strength. Some systems may be better than others as far as swimming is concerned but the evidence as to which is most suitable for swimmers is not conclusive.

GETTING STARTED

Once the equipment to be used has been decided, the next step is to consider what type of exercises should be prescribed to benefit the swimmers.

The coach needs to know something about the muscle groups a swimmer uses to do the various swimming strokes. The added development of physical strength in a muscle group that participates little in swimming movements may well prove detrimental to performance when the actual stroke is done. Perhaps an example of this sort of disparate development occurs when the bicep is isolated and worked for strength. The bicep muscles are little used in swimming.

A selection of useful exercises for developing appropriate swimming muscle groups is illustrated in the following figures. Details on the specific muscle groups primarily worked in each exercise and how added strength in those areas might help swimming performance accompany each illustration. Greater detail on the value of each exercise to swimmers together with further exercises and more stroke-specific weight training will be provided in level III of this course.

ORGANIZATION OF A WEIGHT WORKOUT FOR SWIMMING

Circuit Training

When coaching quite large mixed groups, an excellent way to ensure that everyone does the maximum amount of work in the time available is through the use of circuit training. Circuits can be modified easily to exercise males and females, the different age groups and the specific areas of the body, such as upper-body, abdominals, legs, and so on.

Each exercise point in a circuit is called a station. A circuit can have as many stations as required when setting up a program. A suggested workable circuit consisting of ten stations, using any exercises from those illustrated at the end of this chapter may be organised as follows: — (see page 67).

Patterns of Exercise for the Circuit

Using the exercises illustrated at the end of this chapter (weights or callisthenics or both) as a resource pool, it is possible:

1) to work various muscle groups on the overload principles as shown in the sample circuit (page 67) or

2) Use exercises that involve the different muscle groups used in swimming by organizing the circuit so that each station exercises a different area of the body (refer resource pool at end of chapter).

It can be seen that the coach can design the program to fit any specific shortcomings seen in the team.

Whether the coach wants to prescribe weights, free exercises; develop basic strength and endurance (probably better-suited to the very young in the program); develop specific strength; use fixed apparatus, etc...about the only limitation to the variety and effectiveness of circuit training rests in the coach's ability to use imagination. The important point is that almost any type of exercise can be adapted to a circuit program.

TWO MAIN APPROACHES TO IMPROVING STRENGTH IN SWIMMERS

Currently, there are essentially two philosophies on weight programs for strength gains in swimmers.

Stated simplistically, one claims in essence that by **a)** increasing the weight used by the swimmer to near maximum, **b)** reducing the number of repetitions of the exercise, and **c)** doing the exercise slowly, greatest strength gains will be evident. The other claims that **a)** by using light weights, **b)** by increasing the number of repetitions and **c)** by doing the exercise at a high rate of speed, adequate strength and good endurance gains will result.

At this stage, research does not state decisively which is the best method for increasing strength and power specific to swimming. There seems to be some question at present whether or not there is an optimal level of physical strength that can benefit swimmers.

A HEAVY WEIGHT CIRCUIT

Obviously, there are great risks inherent in using heavy weights with swimmers. If the coach feels the risk of injury to the swimmers is too great, heavy weight should not be used. Since the weights are very heavy, there is increased risk of dropping the weights on one's self or someone else. Warm-up to prevent injury from muscle tear becomes more important. **The coach should ensure swimmers warm up thoroughly before attempting any weight work. Warm-up is part of any strenuous physical activity**. However, since there is strong evidence to show that the only way to become really strong is through the use of heavy weights, the coach should prescribe this type of training for a trial period. **An evaluation of the heavy weight program carried out for a short time will give some insight into their value in each individual program.**

Advocates of heavy weight training believe strength only should be developed out of the water and that power (strength x speed of movement) should be developed in the water.

IMPORTANT:—

In prescribing a heavy weight circuit, more time should be allocated for completing the circuit.

The reasons for allocating more time are as follows:

1. **Adequate time for warm-up is necessary to prevent muscle injuries.**

2. **Because greater concentration is needed to move heavy weights, a preceding period to obtain a "mind set" is needed.**

AN EXAMPLE OF A TEN-STATION-CIRCUIT

1. Bench Press
(Primarily exercises the shoulders, chest and back of the upper arms.)

2. Bent lateral raise
(Primarily exercises the shoulders, upper back, neck and lower chest.)

3. Upright rowing
(Primarily exercises the shoulders, upper back and back of the arms.)

4. Arm Rotator
(Primarily exercises upper and lower chest, shoulders and middle of the back.)

5. Squat Thrusts
(Primarily exercises the gluteal muscles (buttocks), thighs, upper and lower calfs.)

6. Straight arm pullover
(Primarily exercises the shoulders, chest, middle back, under the arms and back of the upper arms.)

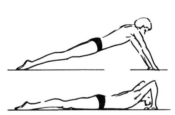

7. Push ups
(Primarily exercises shoulders, chest, lower and upper arms and back of the upper arms.)

8. Jump starts
(Primarily exercises thighs, gluteals (buttocks), biceps and shoulders.)

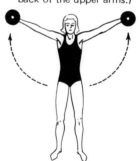

9. Standing lateral raise
(Primarily exercises the shoulders and the back.)

10. Bent arm pullover
(Primarily exercises the shoulders, chest, under arms and back of the upper arms.)

NOTE:—The circuit site could be in a gymnasium, a hall, on the pool deck...or almost anywhere. The above selection of exercises for a sample ten-station-circuit is designed to develop upper-body strength in the swimmer. It should be noted that "relief" exercises are inserted at stations (5) and (8). "Relief" exercises, in this context, are exercises inserted into the circuit to provide a "rest" for a muscle group which is being overloaded.

3. Longer intervening rest periods are needed between repetitions; otherwise the accumulative effects of fatigue may result in difficulty in maintaining the correct form and pattern of an exercise.

In prescribing a heavy weight circuit, the coach should plan carefully the allocated time for completing the circuit to ensure that all the above factors receive consideration.

For heavy weight training circuits it is necessary to create more than one circuit. This is done by grouping swimmers into circuits according to their levels of strength and irrespective of sex or age. Males and females might work with the same weights: ten-year-olds may work with thirteen-year-olds and so on.

A problem with creating more circuits is that more equipment is needed. This means greater expense to the club. Not all clubs can manage to meet the extra costs involved. This is when "do it yourself equipment" becomes a necessity. If a club is fortunate enough to have a good range of commercially-built equipment, the need for extra circuits to allow for strength differences among swimmers can be met. With most modern equipment the weight to be worked against can be changed up or down simply by turning a knob or moving a key or by some other simple means.

Value of the Heavy Weight Circuit

If the increased risk factor, inherent in handling heavy weight, can be coped with and all safety precautions have been taken, this program has particular value to the club program as follows:

1) Experimental evidence shows that the use of heavy weight workouts is the quickest and best way to increase strength.

2) With male swimmers it is possible to achieve a high level of motivation to do them well. The increase in muscle bulk and the related strength gains for most males is very desirable.

In the practical club situation the same value has not been shown to apply to female swimmers. There is a little research evidence to show these differences do exist between males and females in their feelings towards using heavy weights. In the club situation this problem has proved to be a real one.

Finding a Suitable Weight for the Heavy Weight Circuit

A question which might be asked in relation to the heavy weight program is, "How do I arrive at a suitable weight to use for circuit work and how many repeats should I have my swimmers do at each station?" In swim clubs this is a problem since a coach has to work with all ages and sexes, and there will be wide variations in the individual strengths of members. By creating nearly equal strength groups as suggested earlier this problem can largely be overcome.

However, there is still the problem of finding weights suitable for use at each station. One way of finding a suitable weight to work with at each station is as follows. Using the **weakest** member of the circuit group, select a weight with which the swimmer can manage to do just 6 - 8 repetitions. The same number of repetitions is used to decide all station weights in the circuit. Once the weight for each station is decided, a decision has to be made on the number of repetitions that should be done at each exercise point. A common practice in this type of circuit work is to ask swimmers to complete three circuits in say 20 minutes. If this method of working the circuit is followed, to arrive at the number of repeats at each station, the coach simply halves the maximum number of repetitions the weakest member was able to do. In the above example, each swimmer would complete 3 - 4 repetitions at each station. **That is, if the swimmer completes two full circuits in a workout, he/she will have worked to the maximum repetitions for each weight at each station. Of course, the coach may have the swimmers complete any number of circuits. However, the completion of two circuits is a normal workout period used by most coaches, who use circuit-training.**

As strength gains are made by the members of the team, the circuit can be made progressively more difficult to complete by:

1. manipulating the time to complete three circuits. The coach might ask for three times around in 19 minutes;

2. increasing the weight used at each station by small increments;

3. increasing the number of repetitions at each station;

4. increasing the number of circuits to be completed in a given time;

5. increasing the number of circuits to be completed and reducing the time allowed to complete them. That is...doing more work and increasing the intensity of the workload.

A LIGHT WEIGHT CIRCUIT

In this type of exercise circuit any light weight is selected that can be handled with only a little effort on the part of each team member. The selected weight usually can be decided by a method similar to that used for finding the weight suitable for each station on the heavy weight circuit. However, rather than use the weakest member of the group to set a standard, experience has found it is probably better to select someone who is about average for the group. If the coach wants to group the team according to strength, this is quite permissible. However, this is not as critical as it is when using heavy weights since the swimmers:

1)   are not working at the upper limits of their strength capacity.
2)   beneficial workouts for everyone are possible with this arrangement, even though the selected weight for each station may be lighter for some than for others.

This type of circuit is based on the concept of speed repetitions. Variations in the strength of team members is not a critical factor. The stronger swimmer will do more repetitions in a given time than a weaker or younger swimmer and, as a result, do more work For example, swimmer A, in a 30 second time period, may do 30 repetitions. Swimmer B, in the same given time, might achieve 40 repetitions with the same weight. To complete a circuit, the coach may set a schedule of 30 seconds on repetitions with a ten second changeover time to move to the next station. The coach calls "go" for the commencement of each exercise and "change" when the exercise period is complete.

Difficulty in this circuit is increased:

1)   **by manipulating the number of times around the circuit each swimmer will go;**
2)   **by trying for a higher number of repeats at each station;**
3)   **by increasing the weight but still leaving it relatively light;**
4)   **by decreasing the changeover time from station to station;**
5)   **overloading the muscle groups by including in the circuit a number of consecutive exercises that work the same areas of the body.**

Resting

At the end of a "set" of circuits (or only one circuit if so decided) there should be a rest period before doing another set. **The rest should not be longer than two minutes since the body tends to cool too**
much over longer periods

One important point to remember in exercise involving weights with repetitions is that research has shown that muscle damage almost always occurs within the first three to four repetitions of an exercise if it is to occur at all. For this reason, even though a circuit might be based on speed repetitions, the first three repeats should be somewhat slower to reduce the risk of muscular or other injury.

Value of the Light Weight Circuit

The light weight circuit is particularly valuable as a means of improving strength when the group consists of both males and females, has a wide range of age and size and the coach is working with large numbers. Essentially, how much work one does is dictated by the committment and motivational levels of the swimmers doing the circuit.

Another value of this type of circuit, supported by some research, is that high speed work with light weights increases strength as well as endurance. In addition, speed and strength are components involved in the production of power. As the ability to generate power seems basic to success, many believe these gains have a direct positive transfer to actual swimming. This argument is compelling but has not been shown by research to be either true or false.

THE HEAVY WEIGHT WORKOUT OR THE LIGHT WEIGHT WORKOUT

It should be noted that the underlying difference in the philosophy between those who prefer **light weights and high speed repetitions** to those who prefer **heavy weights done slowly with low repetitions** as the best method of improving swimming strength is as follows:

The former believe the ability to generate power is developed **out** of the water and that the transfer to swimming occurs automatically. The latter believe **only** the strength component of power is developed **out** of the water. Speed of movement, the other component of power, is developed by combining the strength gained **out** of the water with the actual stroke pattern **in** the water. They maintain that strength gained through heavy weights is potentially greater than through the use of light weights. They claim that power-increases thus developed are more specific to the swimming stroke-pattern. This is a forceful argument neither proved nor disproved by research.

TECHNIQUE OF EXERCISE

It is mandatory, whether the coach chooses to prescribe heavy weights or light weights or callisthenics, that **all exercises be completed with good form.** In this way, muscle strength is developed through a full range of movement...a basic requirement for good swimming. Some modern apparatus enables close emulation of the stroke pattern actually used in the water. Using this type of equipment, there appears to be quite a large transfer from out-of-the water movements to the actual swimming style. Similarly, any errors, even the most subtle, reinforced by constant repetition on a machine, can be transferred to the swimmer's stroke-pattern.

HOW MUCH WEIGHT WORK SHOULD BE DONE?

The simplest and most straightforward answer is as often as the coach judges it to be needed. This, of course, is not a very satisfactory answer. On this point, again research does not help much. **However, there is evidence that, if the coach decides to prescribe a heavy-weight program, there should be at least one full day rest before working the same muscle groups again.** Obviously, heavy weight training can be done on a daily basis if, for example, one day the coach assigns work on the legs and the next day on the upper body. This sort of cycle can then be repeated.

When using light weight workouts, the above considerations do not seem to be as important. This is because there is not the same severity of exercise with muscles working near the limit as with heavy weight training.

However, irrespective of whether using heavy or light weight training, the coach should be **on the alert** for difficulties such as excessive soreness, tendonitis, etc.

Counsilman (1977) suggests exercises for strength should be done on a daily basis excluding weekends, either before or after workouts. However, as already suggested, a coach can do them as frequently as circumstance requires. At some time of the season it may be best to do as many as seven or eight workouts each week on weights. At other times, workouts may be reduced to as little as two or three a week or even none. Obviously, as important competition approaches,

and freedom from fatigue is an important factor if good performances are to result, the coach might elect to do no weight work. Some highly successful coaches, however, still maintain a light weight program at this stage of their team's preparation.

RELATIONSHIP OF WEIGHT PROGRAM TO THE SWIMMING PROGRAM

A weight program should parallel a swim program in the way it builds up and tapers off. Although this point seems rather too obvious to be stated, it is amazing how many coaches fail to observe it. At peak training periods, the coach probably should be prescribing a weight circuit for about five one hour periods each week...with the weekends kept free to allow for muscular recuperation. **Of course, the number of weight circuit workouts will vary with the frequency and importance of meets.**

Approaching the swimming taper-off (maybe more than one), the weight program also should be tapered off but timed to finish about one week, or a little more, before swimming competition begins. By following this approach, muscular strength will be allowed to reach a peak. Strength seems to be maintainable without further specific weight work throughout as much as one full week or more of swimming competition; provided actual competition is regular in that period. When swimming workouts are resumed and built up, the weight program can also be resumed and built up in the same way.

BODY FLEXIBILITY AND THE WEIGHT PROGRAM

Although methods of developing flexibility will be discussed in detail in another chapter, it is necessary to say a few words about its importance in any weight program aimed at building swimming strength.

The main aim of building strength and power in swimming is to improve performance. This is achieved by increasing power **throughout the range of movement of the stroke patterns.** Attainment of some of the positions required to execute the stroke correctly involves good range of movement in the joints and muscles (flexibility). With increased muscle bulk, which inevitably follows increased strength, these positions, if not practised, become impossible to reach. This decreases the efficiency of the stroke because there is a failure to complete the pattern correctly.

In addition to ensuring that maximum strength is applied in the correct manner to improve swimming

9 PHYSIOLOGICAL BASIS OF TRAINING

Dr. Arend Bonen, Assoc. Professor,
School of Physical Education,
Dalhousie University, Halifax

PHYSIOLOGICAL AND METABOLIC BASIS OF TRAINING PRINCIPLES

A major problem facing every coach is how to use knowledge concerning energy metabolism and basic physiology to produce an effective training program. Table 1 has a summary of changes that occur in the human body in response to proper training procedures. Details of how these changes occur are beyond the scope of this chapter. However, knowledge about the relative importance of aerobic and anaerobic metabolism for different events as shown in Table 1 should guide the coach when devising training programs.

TRAINING PRINCIPLES

1) Overload

Training is based on a few simple ideas. Yet, these are frequently misused. The first training concept is **OVERLOAD**. In the level one manual (An Introduction to Swimming Coaching) OVERLOAD was defined as "a workload greater than that to which the body is accustomed" (p. 98). In practical coaching terms this concept means that if the training is not beyond a certain level no training effects will occur. In other words, it is possible that a training program may not have any effect if not properly done! Or else, a training program may not provide the best effect possible. This also means that if the swimmer does not work hard enough there may be no physiological or metabolic benefit at all. This is totally unproductive and a waste of valuable training time.

2) Progressive Overload

It should also be remembered that the overload must be progressive (PROGRESSIVE OVERLOAD). In other words the workload to which a swimmer is subjected "should be increased gradually and systematically" (level I manual p. 98). The reason that PROGRESSIVE OVERLOAD must be employed is that if the work is kept constant, the swimmer's body will adapt only to that workload. Once this has occurred, the same training load no longer represents an OVERLOAD. Thus, further training adaptation, or conditioning, does not occur since the swimmers physiological and metabolic capacities are no longer OVERLOADED.

3) Specificity

The second concept is **specificity**. As defined in the level one manual (p. 98), "training effects are specific to the type of workload placed upon the body"; therefore, "athletes trained in one sport will require considerable time to adapt to and reach maximum efficiency in another sport." This is even true within the same sport. In other words, for swimmers the conditioning that results is directly dependent on the type of training performed. Therefore the concept of SPECIFICITY dictates that long, slow distance swimming will have little if any effect on the swimmer's improvement over a 100m sprint. Similarly, high quality sprinting (25 - 50m) will do little to improve the swimmer's endurance capacities.

In addition, it should also be realized that while some training programs appear to be highly successful, such success is obtained from having many swimmers in the program. Since some programs violate basic training concepts, a few swimmers may still be successful in spite of the program **not** because of the program. Better designed programs will produce more good swimmers. Since most swim clubs in Canada are relatively small it is critical to develop good, fundamental training procedures in which swimmers will succeed because of the training they are receiving. In poor programs training is merely vicarious.

Among coaches and physiologists the concept of specificity of training is a subject of debate. Certainly in theory the best results may be expected to occur from highly specific training programs. This means the sprinter would only perform sprints and the distance swimmer would only swim distance. From a physiological viewpoint such training should result in the most rapid conditioning for each type of swimmer.

Training for swimming is rarely this simple. First of all a program may have swimmers of all ages and all levels of swimming. These swimmers usually also compete at distances from sprints to distance events. So it may be difficult to select one type of very specific training for even one swimmer.

Highly specific training programs should be applied to the high calibre and/or mature swimmers. These are swimmers who either have **1)** favourite distances in which they do well, or **2)** are excelling at a very high level and need specialized training to bring them to a new level. For such swimmers EVERY METER should be an EFFECTIVE METER. They cannot afford to waste their time on activities of little or no benefit. Swimmers need to train differently for specific events because of the different physiological and metabolic requirements for these events (see Table 1, chapter Eight.

Table 1. Summary of Changes associated with swim training.

ENDURANCE TRAINING		SPRINT TRAINING	
Metabolic Changes	Benefit to Swimmer	**Metabolic Changes**	Benefit to Swimmer
1) increase enzymes for aerobic metabolism	- less reliance on anaerobic energy and fatigue producing substances	1) increase enzymes for anaerobic metabolism	- allows ATP to be formed at more rapid rate and thus may allow the swimmer to contract muscles faster and harder. The result is a faster sprint
2) increased number of open capillaries in muscle	- easier to get oxygen into the muscles		- there may be an increased tolerance for lactic acid
3) increased storage of glycogen in muscle	- increases capacity to perform more repeats or quality swims	2) increase storage of rapid energy sources such as creatine phosphate and ATP	- may permit swimmer to go faster for a longer period of time before fatigue sets in
4) increased number of mitochondria in muscle	- allows more glycogen to produce ATP in presence of oxygen rather than having glycogen produce lactic acid		
Cardiovascular Changes		**Cardiovascular Changes**	
1) increase the amount of blood that can be pumped by the heart	- increases the blood flow to muscles for each beat of the heart	No significant changes	
2) increase the maximal blood flow to the muscles	- as above		
3) lowering of sub-maximal heart rates for a constant workload	- more efficient heart rate for any submaximal swimming speed		
Net Effect		**Net Effect**	
- Combined effects act to allow more energy to be derived from oxygen. This also has the advantage that less lactic acid is built up and thus fatigue processes are delayed. The swimmer ultimately can swim faster.		- There is as yet not too much known about the metabolism and physiology of anaerobic training. However, there appears to be an increased tolerance for lactic acid and a faster generation of energy from anaerobic sources. This should help the sprinter to sprint faster.	

When we are considering young, growing children it may be best to place them on endurance training programs and not to let them specialize. Physiologically young children (under 12 years) cannot build up a lot of lactic acid. This suggests that they may not yet be particularly suited for sprinting activities. There is also a belief that a good swimmer should have a good endurance capacity to swim any distance. This simply allows the swimmer to go faster at any distance without becoming fatigued as fast (in other words less lactic acid is built up). The endurance type of training builds a stronger heart which can deliver more blood and therefore more oxygen to the muscles. This training can also make more of the muscle operate with oxygen. This delays the onset of fatigue. So certainly an endurance base seems physiologically sound and necessary for swimmers.

At present interval training provides probably the best available training procedure. In this type of training a prescribed number of swimming distances are separated by a rest period. The elements of interval training are dealt with in "Introduction to Swimming Coaching" (Level one manual). From a coaching standpoint the interval training method allows the swimmer to practise **longer** and **harder**. This is possible since interval training delays the onset of fatigue, and permits recovery from fatigue. The exact physiology of this is not fully understood and possible explanations are beyond the scope of this chapter.

PHYSIOLOGICAL AND METABOLIC BASIS OF TRAINING PROCEDURES

The purpose of this section is to provide a general physiological background of different training procedures. The procedures are sprint training, distance training, hypoxic training, negative split training. A simple example will be given for each method with a brief physiological and metabolic rationale.

Sprint Training

Training for sprints is physiologically and metabolically demanding and difficult. Rapid improvement in sprinting ability can only be obtained with anaerobic training procedures. With this method the distance to be swum or the time of the swim should be quite short. The distance covered should also be swum "all out", and therefore the rest periods between sets should be long enough to permit a reasonable recovery and hence quality efforts to occur.

The simplest method for anaerobic training is to select a convenient distance which the swimmer can cover in 30 - 50 seconds of all-out swimming. This could be either 50m or 75m swims depending on the stroke. "All out" swims for such short periods of time **with** sufficient rest stresses the anaerobic energy system highly. A likely repeat sequence could be:

4 x 50) with 60 sec. rest
4 x 75) between each repeat   X 4 sets
(ALL OUT SPRINTS!)

Between sets the swimmers may need as much as 10 - 15 min. to recover. Obviously the total distance in such a practice session is not great, **but** it doesn't need to be, since the intensity of the effort is very high. Recovery between sets will be aided by slow easy swimming (1, 2).

Remember that anaerobic training is very stressful. The quality of the swim should be high to obtain an anaerobic effect. Enough rest is necessary to permit good quality swims. The coach should realize that the body needs adequate rest to be able to continue.

Training for 100m

Every competitive 100m distance relies highly on the anaerobic energy system. Training the anaerobic system cannot be done by overdistance swimming. It is best to do underdistance, interval training. This can simulate the sprint very well in swimming time as well as in specific energy metabolism.

The lactic acid system must be stressed highly. To produce such stress the swimmer must swim at top speed for at least 40 to 60 seconds. This stresses the appropriate metabolic system. However, this also produces lactic acid which causes fatigue. Thus, after a few repeats, a reasonable rest (5 - 10 min.) should be allowed, otherwise it would be difficult to maintain good swimming speed. Then the next set of repeats should be performed.

Although sprint training is usually performed in the taper portion of the swimming season, it makes good sense to incorporate it more frequently in the training program. Again, remember that sprint training is very demanding physiologically. It should probably not be done daily, Every other day seems best. The body needs to recover from it. Secondly not much total yardage can be accomplished. This really doesn't matter too much since the effectiveness of training is related more to the intensity of effort (effective meters) rather than the total number of meters performed in a practice.

Effective underdistance training for sprints can enhance sprint performance very specifically. For example, if the coach has a swimmer who is capable of doing 60 sec. for 100m then repeat swims such as 10 x 100 at 1:03 are less effective **than** underdistance sprints. The coach should stress the swimmer at the new desired level, e.g. 58 sec. This may be done by doing 4 x 25 with 2 sec. rest, each 25 in 14.5 sec. Thus, 4 x 14.5 sec. is equivalent to 58 sec. This will provide very good physiological training specificity. **Also**, the right metabolic and physiological systems are stressed.

In summary, sprint abilities are improved with short all-out sprints. These must last about 30 - 60 secs. to stress the correct metabolic system (anaerobic system). This will stress the lactic acid (or "sprint system") of the body. A last point to remember is that such swims must be done very fast to benefit the swimmer.

Effort	100%	95%	95-85%	85-80%	80-70%	65-75%	60-70%
Distance	20-75	100-150	100-150	125-250	150-350	500-1000	1000+
Work Time	10-40 sec	40-70 sec	10-70 sec	1.5-2.5 min	2-5 min	5-10 min	15 min+
Rest Time	5 min	3-5 min	30-60 sec	60-90 sec	30-60 sec	30-60 sec	30-60 sec

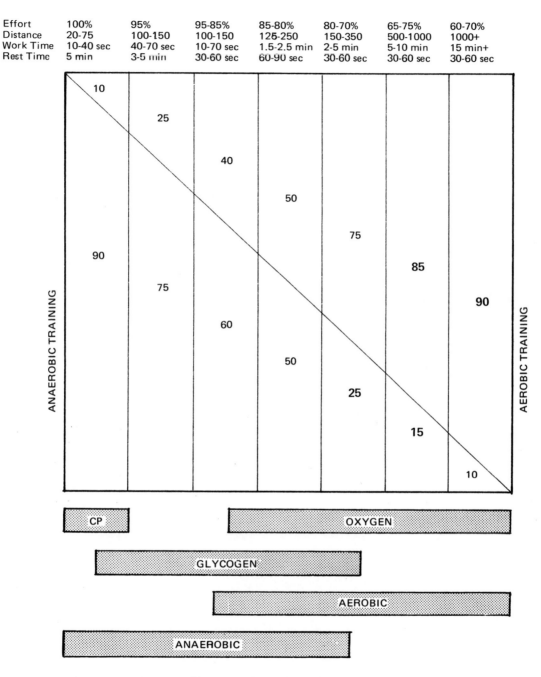

Fig. 1 Summary of Swimming Repetitions in Conjunction with Energy Systems.

This figure illustrates that as Swimming events begin to last longer (going from left to right) there is a shift from anaerobic to aerobic metabolism (see black bars below the figure.) For various swimming distances the relative contribution, in %, of the aerobic and anaerobic contributions are shown. Immediately below this the work time and rest periods are provided which can be used as an aid to train the portion of the metabolic system indicated.

Aerobic Training
Distance or more intensity

Aerobic training is designed to improve oxygen delivery to the working muscles and the ability to use oxygen in the muscle. Most swimming programs stress this system. Swimming programs have progressed from 3,000 m/day in the early 1960's to 8,000 - 20,000 m/day in the 1970's. This is a drastic change in training and time commitment by coaches and swimmers.

Such increases in training distance usually results from swimming many distance repeats with short rests between repeats. It is debatable whether this is the most effective use of training time to produce best results.

The best immediate training effect seems to result from a higher intensity of training. **Increasing the TOTAL DISTANCE** in a practice **is** probably the **least effective** method for obtaining a greater training effect. A more effective means is to progressively improve the quality of the interval swims performed by the swimmer. For example, if the coach prescribes 5 x 400m repeats it is very doubtful that performing 7 x 400m provides a greater training benefit since the extra time required for the 2 x 400 repeats will consume time devoted to other components of the practice. It may be better to increase the training intensity for the 5 x 400m by **a)** swimming each 400 faster than was previously the case and/or, **b)** reducing the rest interval. The combination of **a)** and **b)** is more effective than simply adding an extra 2 x 400m.

Unfortunately, there is no way at present to equate how much intensity improvement is equal to increasing the daily swimming distance. However several research studies conducted on the effects of the intensity, duration and frequency of training have identified intensity as the most critical training variable followed by the frequency and then the duration, (5,6,8), or total yardage in swimming. Further evidence for this is contained in the study by Nordesjo (6). From his study the following three training programs produced similar improvement on a standard laboratory work performance test.

A) 1x/week for 15 min. at all out capacity that could be tolerated for 15 min.
B) 3x/week, 1 hr. per session at 75% effort for that hour
C) 5x/week, 2 hrs. per session at 50% effort for each 2 hr. session.

From the above it can be seen that when intensity is decreased very much more training is necessary to compensate. This means that if the training distance is increased and the intensity of effort consequently decreases, it appears that the swimmer derives less training benefit than before!

Careful judgement should be exercised in changing schedules. Simply increasing total distance may not be the best answer. Certainly increasing the intensity of total practice merits attention, especially since with long training sessions (20,000m) many swimmers are known to just "swim through" them. This may not be an optimal overload, since they are concerned with being able to finish the practices, and not whether they are deriving physiological and metabolic training effects. It is probably quite unnecessary to perform long distance practices of 10,000 - 20,000m per day. Similar benefits can occur with shorter but more quality-oriented training schedules. Conversely, when high intensity training is applied, the swimmer should be observed carefully to avoid failing adaptation. For this reason, training intensity should be applied on a cyclic basis. (Refer to Level One Manual "Introduction to Swimming Coaching".)

Endurance Training

For events of 200m and over the ability to deliver oxygen to the muscles is critical. The more oxygen delivered, the faster the swimmer will be able to go. The oxygen delivery mechanisms were discussed earlier. A significant proportion of training is necessary to improve the oxygen delivery system. This is best accomplished by swims lasting from 2 - 5 min., and occasionally with longer swims. If the swims become much longer than 5 min. intensity may decrease. Thus training for a swim of 10 min. duration might be better accomplished by practising 2 x 5 min. segments with an appropriate intervening rest. This would provide a higher intensity of effort and a better training effect would result. However, if the intensity of effort for the 2 x 5 min. swims is not greater than that of an uninterrupted 10 min. swim there would be no difference in training effect.

A neglected aspect of distance training is often the failure to advise the swimmer of the importance of holding an even pace. If the pace drops off significantly on each repeat the training effect is diminished.

An even pace for events from 200m up is critical. This delays the excessive production of fatigue-producing lactic acid. For example a 400m swimmer capable of doing 5 min., should swim even splits for each 100 meters (for example, 1:13, 1:15, 1:16, 1:16).

If the swimmer has the following splits 1:08, 1:18, 1:20, 1:21, it is obvious the swimmer has gone out too fast. Too much lactic acid is built up and premature fatigue occurs. The result is a poor swim.

Physiologically this poor swim is totally unnecessary. With a controlled even pace there is no danger of premature fatigue...such as would result from swimming the early stages of an event too fast. With an even pace the swimmer has the option of increasing the pace more easily near the end. If the swimmer goes out too fast this option is very difficult. Of course the coach should ensure that the even pace is not a **slow**, even pace!

In workouts even pace swims allow a training specificity for particular events to be developed. If a 5 min., 400 swimmer (1:15 average) wishes to improve to a 4:50 (1:12.5 average) then repeat 100's should be done at the new desired pace.

(*"Splits" is a phrase used to describe intermediate times recorded for any predetermined segment of a racing distance.)

Earlier in the sprint training section it was discussed how 50m and 75m repeats may be used to develop the swimmer's anaerobic capacities. These distances may also be used to improve endurance or aerobic capacities. (See Table 2 for comparison of sprint and endurance programs over the same distances.) This is simply done by providing shorter rest periods **and** by doing many repeats (e.g. 30 x 50 with 5 sec. rests). The swimmer automatically will swim slower when there are many repeats to be done, in comparison to when only a few sprints are performed over the same distance. The metabolic effect with any repeats and a slower swimming speed is that energy is largely obtained from aerobic metabolism. Lactic acid is not accumulated and the swimmer can complete many repeats.

Such repeats, of course, should be performed at or near race pace to derive the training effect specific to the event. The short rest periods probably provide little physiological benefit but the psychology of a brief rest and an encouraging word from the coach cannot be ignored. For example, the physiological

Table 2. Comparison of swimming distances, repetitions and rest periods to build endurance or sprint capacities.

Distance	Examples of Program to build endurance or aerobic energy	Examples of Program to build sprint or anaerobic capacity
25 m	60 x 25 m with 2 sec. rest	4 x 25 (5 sec. rest) x 4 sets - 2 min. rest between sets
50 m	30 x 50 m with 5 sec. rest	4 x 50 m (20 sec. rest) x 4 sets - 5 - 10 min. rest between sets
100 m	30 x 100 m with 5 - 10 sec. rest	3 x 100 m (2 min. rest) x 3 sets - 10 min. rest between sets
200 m	10 x 200 m with 30 sec. rest	3 x 200 m (5 min. rest) x 2 sets - 15 min. rest between sets - limited sprinting benefit
400 m	8 x 400 m with 10 sec. rest	no sprinting benefits for distances of 400 m and up
	Comment - Each repetition in a set should occur at desired race pace.	**Comment** - Swimmer must sprint nearly all out each time for the prescribed distance.

benefits of 20 x 50 with 5 sec. rests are very similar to a 1,000m swim if performed at exactly the same swimming pace. The brief rest can be used advantageously to monitor the pace, or to adjust the pace. It also seems that many swimmers can swim a faster pace with short rests. Therefore, they obtain a better training effect when brief rests are provided during the swim than if a long swim is performed uninterruptedly.

Endurance capacities are improved only when the endurance capacities of the swimmer are stressed. Generally this occurs after about 2 - 3 min. of swimming. Thus the total time for endurance repeats should last at least 2 and preferably 3 min. to obtain repeated aerobic training effects. However, if the swimmer is not expending enough effort, then a 3 min. swim will not provide training effect. In other words a threshold level of effort must be exceeded (OVERLOAD) to obtain a training effect.

The 200m event in swimming is rather unique. This event relies on both the aerobic and anaerobic capacities of the swimmer. Quite clearly a 200m swimmer must train with sprinting and endurance work.

For 200m swimmers 'broken swims' (refer p. 105 Level One Manual — "Introduction to Swimming Coaching") are particularly effective. These simulate the 200 very well, result in high quality efforts, and provide excellent aerobic and anaerobic training effects. Basically such swims can be broken into any combination thereof. For example:

8 x 25m, or 4, x 50m, or 2 x 100m, or
100-50-50, 125-75, etc.

The rest period between segments of such a 200m swim should probably not be any longer than 10 - 15 sec. initially, and can then be reduced during the season to 2 - 5 sec., while maintaining the same pace for the 200 **or** setting a faster pace. This type of 200 swim permits pacing to be developed **and** it stresses the metabolic and physiological systems in such a way as to establish very specific training effects for the 200m events.

USE OF HEART RATE FOR ENDURANCE TRAINING

In the first manual of this series (An Introduction to Swimming Coaching) explanation was provided for monitoring the heart rate either at rest or after swimming (see pages 94 - 95, Level One Manual). The heart rate is a convenient "tool" to assess a swimmer's conditioning process...whether the swimmer is obtaining physiological benefit in any given day of training. Heart rate information is only useful for events that are evenly paced **and** last 2 min. or more. In other words, for events of 200m and higher. The reason for this is that the heart rate for a given swimmer **is** the body's clock which indicates the functioning of aerobic metabolism, **not** anaerobic metabolism.

In events that are quite evenly paced (whether this is in training or in a meet) the heart rate will increase for several minutes and then level off (see figure 2). At the point where it levels off, the heart rate is considered to provide an index of aerobic metabolism and thus the training intensity. This leveling off process is referred to as the **steady state heart rate**. This means that the heart rate is steady because the energy demands by the muscle are now quite constant. If the pace was suddenly increased or decreased the heart rate obviously would also increase or decrease to a new steady state, reflecting changed energy demands (see figure 2).

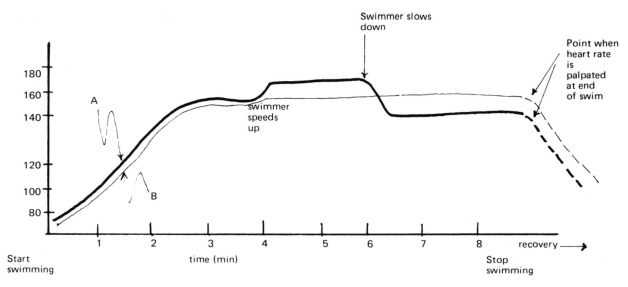

Fig. 2 Heart rate responses during paced (A) and unpaced swimming (B).

When even pace is maintained the heart rate remains stable (Steady-state heart rate). In this case the heart rate taken at the end of the swim is representative of the entire swim. When the pace is uneven the heart rate is also uneven. Therefore the heart rate at the end of the swim only reflects the heart rate over the last part of the swim, not the entire swim.

Experimentally, it has been established that for endurance training the heart rate must exceed 160 beats/min. to obtain any training effect at all in untrained young men. Probably, the heart rates of good swimmers may have to exceed 170 or even 180 beats/min. to obtain a training effect.

In 200 - 1500m swims the heart rate can indicate if the swimmer is **a)** swimming hard enough, and **b)** a training effect is taking place. For events of 200 and over; heart rates at the end of the race (if these could be taken) will usually be in excess of 180 beats/minute. This is because the aerobic system is taxed to near its maximum and therefore the heart rate will be at its maximum which is usually in the range of 180 - 210 beats/minutes.

Individual Differences in Heart Rates

Remember that there are individual differences among swimmers. Some very highly trained athletes may only have a maximum heart rate of 175 beats/min., while others may have maximum heart rates of 190 beats/min. **In general** it is best to remember that

the younger the swimmer the higher will be the maximum heart rate. Thus in 8 - 10 year old swimmers maximum heart rates may be as high as 210 beats/minute. Girls generally have higher heart rates than boys. Thus, if the coach is going to use heart rates as a training index, it is important to recognize the large individual differences in heart rates and determine which swimmers typically have high heart rates.

To determine the swimming heart rate, count the number of beats for 10 seconds immediately after a swim, or teach the swimmer to do this from the pace-clock. Then multiply the 10 second heart beat counts by 6 to obtain the heart rate in beats per minute. To obtain endurance or aerobic training effects it is necessary to **have** heart rates in excess of 160 beats/min. after an evenly paced swim (200m or over). Probably 170 beats per minute is a better general minimum.

The table below is a rough guide for the heart rates one might expect after certain swims. Note also that there is considerable overlap between events to recognize individual differences in heart rates. The heart rates for the 200m events are highest since the swimmer is stressing the aerobic capacity to its maximum and thus the heart rate is at its maximum to provide for the maximum delivery of oxygen. For the 400 - 1500 m events the aerobic metabolism is operating below its maximal capacity and thus the heart rates are slightly lower.

Table 3. Heart rates the coach might expect after swimming certain events.

Event	Expected heart rates at end of race
200 m	190 - 210 beats/minute
400 m	175 - 195 beats/minute
800 m	170 - 190 beats/minute
1500 m	170 - 190 beats/minute

Remember these are only general ranges of heart rates. It is possible to obtain higher or lower heart rates. Also, if the swimmer increases pace in the last 50 or 25 m, the heart rate will rise considerably. This may provide a false indication of how hard the swimmer really worked.

Determine Rest Periods from Heart Rates

In workouts designed to train the aerobic system, the swimmers need to work at certain heart rates for certain periods of time. Thus the heart rate can be a useful training evaluator for endurance training.

The heart rate necessary to improvement in the aerobic energy supply system should generally be in excess of 170 beats/min. Below this level it is doubtful whether much improvement occurs, unless swimming is prolonged for several kilometers.

The heart rate should be maintained at about 170 or higher for 3 minutes or more to stress the oxygen delivery system (the heart). The rest period needs to be only as long as the time needed for the heart rate to recover to about 140-150 beats/min. before the swimmer begins another repeat. (Usually about 1 - 2 minutes, or even less is sufficient.)

Determine Aerobic Training Progress from Heart Rate

Heart rates can also be used to assess the level of the aerobic condition of the swimmer. To do this it is necessary to have the swimmer complete an evenly paced swim. A 400 swim is probably best. The heart rate then is taken at the end as described earlier. Then throughout the season this 400m swim can be repeated. It would be desirable if the swimmer attempted to repeat the same time for each 400m throughout the season (e.g. 4:45), since then the heart rate at the end of each 400m swim should become progressively lower throughout the season. In this way physiological improvements in aerobic capacity can be charted.

It may be difficult to have the swimmer repeat each 400m in exactly the same time throughout the season. In this case a faster 400m swim can indicate an improvement in aerobic conditioning level if the heart rates at the end of each swim are about the same. In other words the swimmer is faster with the same stress on the heart. The example below illustrates these two cases.

		Sept.	Nov.	Jan.	March
Swimmer A	400 m swim time	4:40	4:40	4:40	4:40
	Heart rate	175	165	165	158
Swimmer B	400 m swim time	4:40	4:35	4:30	4:30
	Heart rate	175	173	174	175

For Swimmer A the heart rate decreases from Sept. to Nov. and again from Jan. to March. However, from Nov. to Jan. the heart rate did not change. Physiologically then the training during this period provided only a maintenance load. No physiological improvement was evident.

For Swimmer B the times for each 400m improved from Sept. to Jan. while the heart rate remained about the same even though significant swimming improvement occurred. Therefore, it can be inferred that conditioning has occurred. However from Jan. to March the 400m time had not improved and heart rate was also the same. Therefore training apparently did not change the aerobic level of conditioning.

If Swimmer B had swum the same 4:30 in March but if heart rate had then been 160 instead of the 174, then it could have been concluded that physiological conditioning had occurred, since to swim the same effort in March was accomplished at a lower heart rate than in January.

Remember that, as a swimmer's technique improves, so does efficiency improve. Therefore, the examples for the swimmer's changes in heart rates or swimming times in the above example may be due partially to improved swimming efficiency and not conditioning. It is difficult to separate these two effects without sophisticated laboratory equipment. Nevertheless, for the swimmer an improved level of aerobic condition and/or improved swimming efficiency will result in faster swimming performance.

HYPOXIC TRAINING

This method has been "known" for a long time and has recently been "rediscovered". Hypoxic training means training without sufficient available oxygen (hypo-low; oxic-oxygen; therefore - **low oxygen**). This is done simply by having the swimmer hold the breath every other or every third stroke. It can be dangerous. Unfortunately it is not yet fully understood what causes the body to adapt to training. The idea that training is provoked simply by the lack of oxygen is probably too simple; since with pure anaerobic training, when there is clearly insufficient oxygen available to meet the energy demands of swimming, there is no improvement in aerobic capacity.

There is no doubt that hypoxic training (breath holding) rapidly stresses the swimmer. However, this method is not appropriate for endurance training. Several recent research studies indicate no additional physiological benefits of hypoxic training on endurance capacity. With endurance training a better "hypoxic" effect is obtained by simply making the swimmer swim faster. That is, the intensity of endurance swimming should be increased. This provides a more specific training effect for the physiological and metabolic systems.

For sprint training, hypoxic training may have some benefit. But this is not known for sure. The anaerobic system is stressed in sprint training. A greater stress can be created with hypoxic swimming. **a) This can be dangerous** and **b)** there is no information to indicate that hypoxic training provides additional training benefits. It is speculated that it might.

NEGATIVE SPLIT SWIMMING

"Negative splitting" ("Negative splits" — p. 106 — Level One Manual — "Introduction to Swimming Coaching") is often used as a training method. For example; for a 400m swim the first 200 is slower than the second 200. Physiologically this may provide

additional stress on the aerobic system during the second 200m, since the swimmer must pick up the pace. However, if the first 200m was relatively slow then the physiological training effect of a faster second 200m is lost. Negative splitting is only useful if a normal first 200m pace is held and then extra effort is applied in the second part of the race. This simply requires an extra effort and produces a greater training effect.

In summary, the coach must take care to make every facet of the training program physiologically and metabolically specific. Endurance swims improve endurance capacity and sprints develop sprinting ability. Quite simple, but the simple concepts are frequently lost in the quest for a magic training procedure.

Training is not magic. Swimming requires dedicated, hard work. Hypoxic training and negative split swimming may be useful adjuncts to normal, sound training procedures. However, it is unrealistic to expect that these training devices will make an immediate, dramatic change in swimming performance. Improvements in swimming performances are accomplished by regular, well-planned, fundamental, and high quality swimming practices. Training gimmicks provide an interesting variety in swimming practices... but they cannot replace the basic hard dedicated work required for swimming.

STROKE MECHANICS AND SWIMMING ENERGY

Much of the swimmer's time is spent in training BUT there are limits to how much endurance capacity can be improved. It is doubtful whether the physiological maximal capacity of a swimmer improves much after a rigorous 3 - 5 year training program.

Improvement in swimming performances can also be achieved by improving the stroke-efficiency of the swimmer. This seems to be much neglected in many swim programs where swimmers appear to be pounding out "mindless" metres. Great improvement in swimming times can be obtained, without any improvement in physiological or metabolic training, if swimming mechanics are improved. This is true for almost every swimmer. This would conserve the swimmer's energy for speed.

A good portion of the swimmer's energy or oxygen is spent on overcoming the resistance or drag presented by the water. Poor body position, poor leg position, and wasteful arm movement, all contribute to the energy cost of swimming.

The efficiency for a poor swimmer is about 1%

In other words the poor swimmer must put out 100 units of energy to get 1 unit of useful work. An Olympic swimmer has an efficiency rating of about 5% (for 100 units of energy expended, 5 useful units are produced). Quite obviously a **5X** improvement in efficiency can be obtained from your swimmers. This is a significant improvement!

In practical terms, this means that even taking a swimmer from 2% to 3% efficiency allows that extra 1% to be converted to greater speed. This represents a gain of **50%** in useful swimming speed, since the extra 1% of efficiency is added to the 2% efficiency. More simply stated: for exactly the same energy expended, the swimmer can go much faster if efficiency is improved. **Efficiency in swimming means good stroke mechanics and less fatigue.**

Improvement in swimming speed is obtained from a) **improved conditioning** and b) **improved stroke efficiency**.

All coaches condition their swimmers but good stroke work is often sacrificed for conditioning. A swimmer's speed can be significantly improved by refining stroke mechanics. This is particularly true in swimmers who have been swimming for many years. Further training may not be improving their level of conditioning but rather serving to **maintain** physical conditioning developed over the years. To obtain further improvement, stroke refinement should be an integral part of their training.

REFERENCES

Belcastro, A.N. and A. Bonen. Lactic acid removal rates during controlled and uncontrolled recovery from exercise. J. Appl. Physiol. 39:932-936, 1975.

Bonen, A. and Belcastro, A.N. Comparison of selected recovery methods on lactic acid removal rates. Med. Sci. Sports 8:176-178, 1976.

Campbell, C.J., Bonen A., Kirby, R.L., Belcastro, A.N. Relationship between muscle fiber composition and selected performance tests (In preparation, 1978).

Counsilman, J.E. Competitive Swimming Manual for Coaches and Swimmers. Counsilman Co. Inc. Bloomington, Ind. 1977.

Davies, C.T.M. and Knibbs, A.V. The effects of intensity duration and frequency of effort on maximum aerobic power output. Int. Z Angew. Physiol. 29:299-305, 1971.

Nordesjo, L.O. The effect of quantitated training on the capacity of short and prolonged work. Acta Physiol. Scand. Suppl. 405, 1974.

Nygaard, E., and Nielsen, E. Skeletal muscle fiber capillarization with extreme endurance training in man. International Congress of Swimming Medicine, Stockholm, 1977 (In press).

Shephard, R.J. Intensity, duration and frequency of exercise as determinants of the response to a training regime. Int. Z. angew. Physiol. 26:272-278, 1968.

Recommended reference:

Fox, E.L. and Matthews, D.K. Interval Training. W.B. Saunders Co. 883 Oxford St., Toronto, Ont. M8Z 5T9.
This is an excellent source for the beginning coach to learn about the fundamentals of training with a sound physiological basis. The book is designed for the coach and is easy to read with many examples.

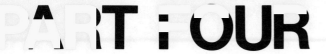

PART FOUR

MOTIVATION

PART FOUR

13

Dr. Murray Smith,
Professor of Physical Education,
University of Alberta, Edmonton

MOTIVATION AS A SYSTEM OF INCENTIVES

WHAT IS MOTIVATION?

The term "motivation" has the same root as motor, meaning "to move". The coach must develop means of understanding what it is that moves, motivates, or provides the drive to maintain both the swimmer's physical efforts and the desire to improve.

We do things because of "what we get out of" the activity, for the "payoff" that we receive for doing it. Payoff in this sense is not restricted to medals, money, or other external rewards but includes all of the consequences that are experienced because of participating. This payoff provides the incentives for putting in the time and effort required.

Birch and Veroff (1966) have identified seven incentive systems that are useful in explaining human motivation. These systems provide a framework that helps in understanding individual motivation and in planning for increasing motivation or tapping new sources of incentives.

The incentive systems are: **sensory, curiosity, achievement, aggressive, affiliative, power, and independence.** These systems almost always overlap and work in combinations of two or three at a time.

Let us describe briefly what each incentive system is and then consider some examples of how they act in combination.

Motivation from the sensory incentive system

To live is to experience the world through our senses: seeing, hearing, tasting, smelling, and touching. Experiences that excite our senses can be stimulating and rewarding. The sights, sounds, smell and feel of a workout or meet will have an impact on the athletes. For some of them it will be an exciting and satisfying experience that attracts and holds them.

The "feel" that comes from cutting smoothly through the water with a powerful, efficient stroke, combined with the sight of churning water, respected teammates and colorful surroundings can have an exhilirating effect. Such a sensory "high" is frequently experienced by athletes and can be part of the payoff which makes the effort worthwhile.

Clean, bright, attractive surroundings including pleasant dressing rooms and good quality water will increase chances that the impact of workouts and meets on the senses of those taking part, will be good.

Pleasant, attractive people who are well groomed and practice good personal health habits will help too.

So will varying the sensory stimulation by changing notice board material, occasionally enjoying a tasty treat such as hot chocolate and donuts after a workout.

Motivation from the curiosity incentive system

Curiosity is a powerful motivator. It often finds expression through questions raised within the athlete. What would it be like to swim well? How fast could I swim? Would it be hard to learn? I wonder which strokes would be best for me? **Wouldn't** it be great to do a fast flip turn like he does? What would it be like to belong to a good team and compete in top swim meets?

Once a person begins to pay attention to such questions, he or she might well be moved to get involved in a club. Such motivating questions can be raised in the minds of potential swimmers by signs or displays, especially with exciting pictures, a little radio or TV coverage of a meet, workout, club member, or some special program the club has underway. "Visitors' day", when swimmers bring a friend to watch and then engage in some easy items. Novelty races or water games also help.

Curiosity also must be put to work for the established swimmer or regular club member. There are many ways to do this but here are a few.
1. Plan to "break the monotony" fairly regularly with "fun things" like novelty items in a workout, pick up races and water games, especially those the kids suggest or always enjoy.
2. Build anticipation. Remember waiting for and wondering about Christmas presents? Plan an item and build anticipation by saying something like, "Boy, have we got something planned for Friday's workout!"
3. If there are any "hams" around, including the coach, encourage them to put on brief skits or give them opportunities to display their antics. One coach wore a rented cat costume to a workout because he had been called a tyrant and he said this would prove he was just a pussycat. The kids loved it.
4. Most important of all, take time to vary workouts so that swimmers do **not** know what to expect next. Nothing kills curiosity like dull routine. Look for different ways to practise skills and change the order of workouts so that there are surprises in what comes next.

The important thing is to do surprising, unexpected things every now and then, so that curiosity is maintained through a what-will-happen-next? attitude.

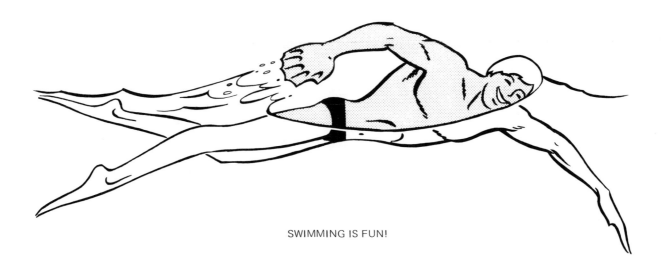

SWIMMING IS FUN!

In a more serious way the coach can call on curiosity by posing questions to the swimmers. What do you think are your best four events right now? Do you think you could average 50 seconds on this set?

By avoiding dull routine and doing things that make swimmers ask questions or think carefully, one can tap the incentive power of curiosity.

Motivation from the achievement incentive system

When one sets or accepts a goal and then sets out to meet that goal, the achievement incentive system is in operation.

One can set goals in two distinct ways.

External goals are those that exist "outside" the athlete. A Canadian or world record may be the external goal of some swimmers. A time standard for entry into a particular meet might be another. Medals or championships are others.

Internal goals are those which the athlete sets or accepts internally or "inside" himself. These goals often have to do with past performance. For example, the swimmer may note that he or she is able to do a certain set during workout faster than was possible the month before. They may be able to complete 1000 meters more in an hour-and-a-half workout than at the same time one year ago.

When swimmers become motivated to improve their effectiveness, to become more efficient, more competent, the achievement incentive system is almost certainly in operation.

HARD GOALS/EASY GOALS

This is the incentive system that is the real key to success. Setting realistic goals and seeing real evidence of progress towards those goals is essential. Nothing succeeds like success! It is true, however, that the achievement motive usually works in combination with other motives, and some of these combinations will be discussed later.

The achievement motive is closely related to what the swimmer aspires to do — how high he shoots. The level of aspiration and some of its effects on achievement motivation will be discussed in a later section.

Motivation from the aggressive incentive system

Aggression can be expressed by attacking people physically (fighting or beating) or by attacking verbally (calling them names). The nature of swimming is such that physical aggression is not part of the sport although it certainly is part of water polo. The standard of conduct required in swimming does not allow verbal aggression either.

It is no doubt true that some swimmers are motivated to a degree by aggression. Although they may not lash out physically to hurt an opponent, or let go with a stream of insults, they often find themselves with an attitude that says, "Come on, do your best, and I'll whip you in the water. I'm better than you, and I'll prove it!"

There have been a good many attempts to prove that man is naturally and unavoidably aggressive. The evidence is far from convincing and those interested in reading up on this matter could begin with the paperback, **Man and Aggression**, by Ashley Montague. (Published by Oxford University Press, 1973.)

There is a great deal of evidence to support the idea that all of us learn how to express aggression, and to control it, from the adults around us, particularly those who are important or significant in our lives — parents, teachers, coaches.

When a coach encounters a particularly aggressive swimmer, every effort should be made to help him learn to control the aggression and express it without being destructive.

Motivation from the affiliative incentive system

Affiliative means to "receive on friendly terms". The kind of warm, friendly, association we often see among people on the same team is evidence of the affiliative incentive system at work. Human beings are social animals, they need to feel that they belong to groups which both give them strength and help them to identify themselves.

When we feel anxious or threatened it is reassuring to have others around to help us understand what is going on and to help protect us. We also need the approval of others in what we say, how we say it, how we act and dress, and what we think is important. Grou set standards of behavior, dress, and performance. These standards become the norms of the group.

Often a top swim team has a tradition (longstandir norms or behavior objectives) of hard work, fun, and coming through in big meets. To be truly accepted by such a team, new members must be prepared to accept these norms, these traditions. By doing so, young people get help in identifying themselves: I'm a Shark. We are tough to beat! We work hard but have lots of fun. We concentrate and put all we've got into every race! It's great to be a Shark!

Research on motives of athletes indicates that the affiliative motive may be the strongest and most common one in operation. While it is possible to becom preoccupied with trying to win approval from the group this does not happen too often. When it does the coach should point out to such a swimmer, in private, that the real way to win a secure place in the group is by working hard and joining in the fun in a natural way.

Contrary to what might be expected, people who need approval from the group are not any more easily led than more independent people. Very often, prestige within the group will come to the person who shows some leadership or speaks up on an issue and turns the thinking of the group around to a new direction.

Some reasonable time and attention should be given to generating a genuine team "spirit". Setting out club rules, taking pride in how workouts are run, in behavior and performance at meets, and having social get-togethers, can generate a strong feeling of what the club stands for. Once this feeling is established it will become a powerful influence in holding the swimmers, coaches, and other adult members together.

Motivation from the power incentive system

Power is defined as being able to influence the decisions of other people. The coach has a good deal of power since he can make many decisions that influence swimmers and others associated with the club.

Children ordinarily have very little power. In fact a good many of them spend a lot of time trying to defend themselves against those who have power over them. While power may be used forcefully such as hitting, spanking, confining one to his or her room, it may also be used more subtly. A shake of the head, an upheld hand, silence, and other cues are often very quietly used to control behavior. So might the withdrawal of privileges or rewards be threatened or used if the swimmer fails to behave as desired.

While it is true that the young swimmer especially must have many decisions made for him, or her, there are things that should be left under their control. Many coaches know how difficult it is to deal with children whose parents want them to swim but who do not themselves want to do so. Such children exercise **their power** by dallying in the locker room, having to be forced into the water, failing to concentrate on technique, rest intervals, or repeat times.

The degree of coersion that justifiably can be used as power over swimmers is a complex problem that cannot be discussed in detail here. What is important at this point, is finding ways to give the swimmer some legitimate power of his or her own. If coaches and parents are willing to reserve their power for really important uses, they will be able to find many ways in which swimmers can make certain decisions and thus retain some power of their own. For example, especially for younger children, some workouts should be optional and those to be missed should be selected by the swimmer.

Within workouts, especially early in the season, some items on the schedule should be optional and may be left out at the discretion of the swimmer. Some other items (only those so designated by the coach) may be reduced up to a given percent. That is if an item called for 20 x 50 repeats, the coach might indicate that swimmers could choose to do only 16 x 50, if desired, or rest time could be variable from say 10 to 20 seconds.

Note that it is not intended that such flexibility be offered every workout, or on all items. But the variety and having some chance to make decisions will often have a very stimulating effect on swimmers.

Swimmers of all ages and stages should have some say in what meets they do **not** enter and what events they **do** enter. Of course, sometimes swimmers will want to enter meets and events that are over their heads or that are already filled by more competent teammates. Here the coach's decision may well have to stick. But rarely should a coach insist that a swimmer enter a meet or race that he or she has strong objections to. This may be necessary **very rarely** but if it becomes a regular thing it almost certainly means that coaches and/or parents are using their power unwisely.

If swimmers are allowed to make some significant decisions they will be less likely to feel that they are being pushed around needlessly. Furthermore, if parents and coaches expect swimmers to be able to make sensible decisions, they must allow the young people some continuing practice in doing so. Swimmers who can exercise power over their own lives will have an additional source from which to draw valuable motivation.

Motivation from the independence incentive system

Independence refers to the ability to accomplish something without help. Young people of course need a good deal of help in many ways from many sources. It is probably easier to do things for youngsters than to offer only that assistance that is needed and stand back at crucial times so that the younger person may learn on their own.

The best coaches learn to "help out of the way" at times and wait for requests to help. In this way a mature independence in the swimmer can be fostered. One cannot expect independent young people, who can "stand on their own two feet", unless the growing up **process includes a good deal of graduated** decision-making. Graduated, in this sense means to be given a little freedom to make decisions at first and then a little more and still more as the swimmer learns to make judgements for him or herself.

Some children are more mature and able to make sensible decisions quite early while others, often because they are not allowed reasonable independence, are very late in getting to this kind of maturity, or may never reach it.

If the incentive system of independence is to help motivate swimmers, then they must be given opportunities to make decisions regarding themselves and help in developing sound judgement. They will also need to be rewarded for showing increased independence. Notice the relationship between power and independence. The more power others have over us, the less independent action is open to us, and vice versa. An effective coach will strike a healthy balance between exerting his power and allowing the swimmer independence. This has already been discussed to some degree in the section above.

Coaches interested in having swimmers become more independent should avoid "spoon-feeding". Rotating assignments such as putting in lane ropes, getting out kick-boards or hand paddles will help teach that these routine tasks are to be shared. You do your part in turn and then enjoy independence while others do their part.

Asking questions which focus the swimmer's

attention will help him learn to take over control of his own actions rather than maintaining a situation in which the coach is always responsible for everything. In stroke technique such questions might be: When you breathe (in freestyle) are you lifting your head? Should you be? In breaststroke, are you kicking one foot and lower leg deeper than the other? In your butterfly, how many downbeats of your legs are there in each full arm cycle and where are your arms in their cycle when the downbeats occur?

Pace is a critical skill in swimming. Good pace is the result of the swimmer's independent action. The coach should help the swimmer develop this independence during workouts and pre-race warmup.

One procedure that can be used in teaching pace is to ask a swimmer for "predicted time" swims in which 80% - 90% efforts are swum with a specific time in mind. Soon predicted times with predicted splits can be swum quite accurately.

In setting pace, during a pre-race warmup, have the swimmer set target times for a 25, 50 or 100. After completing the swim, request the swimmer to say to the nearest tenth what the recorded time was. Then tell the swimmer whether the time estimate was right or wrong. After adequate practice of this method, the swimmer will become very accurate at estimating pace. This will result in high quality swims at precise paces.

When first focusing on use of the clock or watch do not expect accuracy. Reward swimmers for paying attention to the clock and assure them that they will soon develop accuracy. This is why keeping an accurate daily log of workout times and items will be beneficial. Such a log will help swimmers recall times and "build in their own clock" that will be a sign of independence and maturity in a positive direction.*

Combinations of incentives in motivation

While it is helpful to separate and discuss the **seven incentive systems** outlined above, it will be obvious that they often act in combinations in any one swimmer at a given moment.

While watching an enthusiastic young swimmer thoroughly enjoy a tough workout, one might well be seeing a mix of **sensory, achievement, affiliative**, and **independence** motivation in operation. The clear sky, sparkling water, and slick feel of powerful stroking, provide a **sensory** stimulus.

Perhaps the set being swum is going very well

*Refer Page 96, Level One Manual ("Introduction to Swimming Coaching, Cecil Colwin.)

with repeat times excellent and improved stroke mechanics under control. These provide a real sense of **achievement**. The comradeship of trusted and respected teammates and coaches provide deep **affiliative** satisfaction. The awareness the coach is there is needed but the swimmer understands what is to be done and gets on with the job. A growing sense of **independence** is being developed.

Perhaps the lively boy, resting 30 seconds between repeats, day-dreams about what it will be like next week at a meet in another province and smiles at the satisfaction he experiences in proving how fast he is. He might even think about how the only way he could get that satisfaction before was to beat up his rivals.

The motivational systems of human beings are complicated and unpredictable. These systems can never be fully understood. **If the coach observes swimmers carefully, listens to them sincerely, encourage their opinions the coach will begin to get valuable insight into what combinations of incentives will motivate individual swimmers**.

Extrinsic and intrinsic motivation

Just as external goals are outside the swimmer, extrinsic (meaning external) motivation arises outside the swimmer. Records, medals, trophies, championships, travel, a club jacket or sweatsuit, these are all extrinsic motivators. So is a parent's desire or coach's desire if that is what keeps a swimmer going.

Adults are often in a position to interfere with the incentive systems of children in order to get the children to do as they want them to. All of us who have been or are parents or coaches have done this.

For example, if a father wants his son to swim he can threaten him by withholding his approval of the boy, defeating the boy's need for affiliative feelings towards the father. Or he can withhold presents such as a motorbike or trip to the lake to waterski, both of which deny him sensory excitement and perhaps challenge feelings of superiority (aggression) over other team members who do not have motorbikes or never get to waterski.

Sources of motivational drive

It is not possible to clearly identify where the incentive patterns we observe in people really come from. We can be sure however that all higher animals require and seek sensory stimulation, engage in exploratory play and other activity that is motivated by curiosity, and are willing to spend a lot of time mastering certain aspects of their environment. Under